Nicole Gonzalez was raised in a small town in central New Jersey. Nicole is a wife, a mother of two beautiful children, and has backpacked through dozens of countries around the world. Nicole has always been passionate about reading and writing, which led to her career as an educator. Nicole encourages everyone to pursue traveling, soak up the world, and dive into personal growth at an early age. *The Book Every Teen Should Read* is Nicole's first book and acts as a guide to help teens navigate their lives and develop a sense of self-worth, positive mindset, and personal values.

D1472932

To all the teens who have inspired me more than
you'll ever know.

Nicole Gonzalez

THE BOOK EVERY TEEN SHOULD READ

Discovering your self-worth, positive mindset, and personal values

AUSTIN MACAULEY PUBLISHERS™

LONDON • CAMBRIDGE • NEW YORK • SHARJAH

Copyright © Nicole Gonzalez 2023

All rights reserved. No part of this publication may be reproduced, distributed, or transmitted in any form or by any means, including photocopying, recording, or other electronic or mechanical methods, without the prior written permission of the publisher, except in the case of brief quotations embodied in critical reviews and certain other non-commercial uses permitted by copyright law. For permission requests, write to the publisher.

Any person who commits any unauthorized act in relation to this publication may be liable to criminal prosecution and civil claims for damages.

Ordering Information
Quantity sales: Special discounts are available on quantity purchases by corporations, associations, and others. For details, contact the publisher at the address below.

Publisher's Cataloging-in-Publication data
Gonzalez, Nicole
The Book Every Teen Should Read

ISBN 9781638297635 (Paperback)
ISBN 9781638297642 (ePub e-book)

Library of Congress Control Number: 2022923329

www.austinmacauley.com/us

First Published 2023
Austin Macauley Publishers LLC
40 Wall Street, 33rd Floor, Suite 3302
New York, NY 10005
USA

mail-usa@austinmacauley.com
+1 (646) 5125767

Thank you to the team at Austin Macauley Publishers who took a chance on *The Book Every Teen Should Read*. It is no easy task to take a chance on a brand-new author, but you believed in me and I thank you for your hard work in bringing my dream to life.

I'd like to shout out to my students, both former and future. Watching you chase your dreams and head off into an unknown world is unbelievably inspiring.

Thank you to all my siblings and sibling-in-laws. There are so many of you, and somehow, you all love and support me unconditionally. Thank you, Kristen Coyne, Alexa Gonzalez, Melissa Cartlidge, and Brendan Cartlidge, for your valuable insight. The book wouldn't be the same without you.

And finally, I want to save the biggest thank you for last. Thank you to my husband, Christian Gonzalez, for your never-ending love and support. I pitch you many of the wild and crazy dreams I have, and you encourage me to pursue them every time. Thank you for your support in publishing this book. I couldn't have done it without you.

won't let any diagnosis define you because it doesn't. You are who you are—not your anxiety or your depression or your ADHD or your addiction or any other thing you might be experiencing. That diagnosis is likely not forever and it's totally normal to experience it. In fact, according to Mental Health First Aid, almost half of the United States' adult population (46.4%) experiences some kind of mental illness in their lifetime. So you are *not* alone. But we'll get more into this too, don't worry.

Regardless of your situation, I'm thrilled that you're here. I'm eternally grateful that you've put your trust in me and I hope during our time together, we'll become close friends.

I'm willing to bet that most of you haven't read personal growth books before, so I'm buzzing with excitement to get you started on this journey. I applaud you for every challenge you take on and always remember that you're not alone in this journey.

In 2019, there were 15.3 million students enrolled in high school in the United States. That number blew my mind. That's more than our country's population size in the early 1800s! I know that was a long time ago, but still, we didn't surpass that number until the 1840s.

That's a crap ton of you teens in high school right now. And so what does that mean? That means you're not alone. Even if you have days when you feel alone, I promise you, you're not.

So cheers to you, you wonderful, fiery, amazing, zealous, fun, determined, wild, loving, curious teens! The world is yours for the taking, my friends. I am thrilled to be here with you.

Chapter 1
Your Feelings Are Valid

Have you ever peed your pants before?

Yes, that's a serious question. I'll ask you one better: have you ever peed your pants *at school* before? If you have, you remember what a horrible day that was.

Now picture this: you come home from a bad day at school (quite literally, a really bad day because you just peed your pants) so you just want to crawl into your bed for the rest of the day. But instead of sleeping, your parents barge in and ask what's wrong. And then when you tell them that you peed your pants and how you're feeling embarrassed and frustrated, they say something like, "It's OK. Don't feel sad. You have a great life. You should feel happy."

And then they leave you on your bed feeling even worse because now you think you should feel better but you still feel crappy so it's like a double crap load of feelings.

It's wild. And that kind of thing happens all the time. Maybe not the same situation (let's hope you don't pee your pants all that often) but hey, we've all had an accident before!

It's also wildly confusing, because I don't blame your parents for wanting to be comforting. The thing is, most of us aren't taught how to comfort someone else. Your parents think they're doing the right thing by trying to comfort you.

Truth is, they're just doing a bad job of it and they don't even know it.

Now replace your parents in the story with your siblings or your friends or your teachers or anyone else who's tried to comfort you.

As a society, we often tell people how they should feel and then we pat ourselves on the back because we think we're helping. It's so wrong! And I don't know why this hasn't been a bigger topic by now.

When people are hurting, we can't be so quick to tell them how they should feel. If someone's feeling crappy, then let them feel that way. I came to this discovery when I was doing my own soul searching, and I believe it's so powerful that it should be taught to the youth: Focusing on someone else is stealing away from their human experience.

When we tell someone else how to feel, we're stealing away from their human experience.

So now, if you are ever in a bad mood and someone tells you how you should feel, politely tell them that they're stealing away from your human experience. I bet you'll blow their minds. The thing is, they've probably never heard that before. But this will be a polite way to tell them "Hey, I'm allowed to feel this way."

And I think you should. Because when we tell people to stop feeling sad and to get back to a state of being happy then we're not letting them manage their own emotions. Instead, we're convincing them to suppress their emotions and keep them hidden or bottled up. We're basically saying, "your feelings aren't valid and that you shouldn't feel that way."

So many of you teens are taught to bottle up your emotions. Your emotions then fester causing unrelenting anxiety and depression. The World Health Organization actually tells us that depression is the leading cause of global disability.

Don't you teens want to change that narrative? Don't you want to be the generation that rises to the occasion and tells anxiety and depression to shove it?

I bet you do.

And I want to help you to do it.

And the first way to start is by accepting your emotions. Stop pressing them further down into your stomach. Stop letting people tell you to "get back to a state of feeling happy" or "just feel better" or simply to feel anything else for that matter. Whatever emotions you're feeling is OK. And you need to feel them in order to overcome whatever it is that you're going through.

My friends, your feelings are valid.

You Have Permission

It's sad to think when I was in high school that I would judge myself for feeling a certain way. I often judged myself when I was feeling sad or pain or grief or anger. I felt like it was wrong to feel those emotions, which triggered other emotions like shame and humiliation. I would actively try to hide the way I was feeling or push them aside.

We have formed an association with optimism and positivity being the way everyone should feel at all times. And if you feel anything else, then it's the wrong way to feel.

If your friend lies to you, you should stop being so angry and get back to being happy.

If you go through a break-up, you should stop being sad. There's plenty of fish in the sea.

If you fail a test, then you should stop feeling ashamed. Work harder next time.

The list goes on and on.

Your friends, your loved ones, your parents, your teachers, and everyone around you probably encourage you to stop feeling a certain way and just be positive all the time.

You guys, this is wrong!

Wouldn't it be really freaking weird if we just felt super positive all the time?

The reality is, it's unrealistic. And it's unsustainable. We all feel a range of emotions every single day and it's not fair to only acknowledge a few of them. When we suppress other emotions, they tend to grow stronger and stronger.

It's almost like when you want a brownie, but your mom tells you no more sweets before bedtime. But there they are, freshly baked hot fudge brownies right in front of your eyes. The longer they sit there and the more you stare at them, the more you want to eat them.

Your emotions are the same way. The longer they sit there and the more you ignore them, the stronger they get.

So here's my suggestion to you: stop fighting your emotions.

Welcome your feelings with open arms and know that you're allowed to feel that way. Stop suppressing your emotions, stop ignoring your feelings, and understand that they're giving you the full human experience.

It's not only fair to feel your emotions but it's necessary in order to understand those feelings. I want you to know that you have permission to feel however you want to feel. Your feelings are valid. They always have been regardless of what you've been told.

Don't Blame Genetics

Genes get blamed for way too much these days. We've associated genetics to be the reason we feel certain things.

"My mom is so emotional, I guess I got that from her." Or;

"My dad's always had a short temper. I definitely got that from him."

While it is true that we learn response mechanisms from our parents, it's not our genetics that inherently cause us to respond. We have the ability to learn different behaviors and other strategies to manage our emotions.

Our lifestyle and the decisions we make play a large role in how we express our emotions. Our environment and the space we live in also play a critical part.

Today, with all of the technology and tools at our fingertips, we must be strong and empowered to push aside the distractions and create a healthy environment for our emotions.

For the teen whose father has a short temper, make sure you're expressing your emotions daily. Find ways to manage stress like running, writing, playing music, kickboxing, taekwondo, etc. (We'll dive into this in more detail later.) And for the teen whose mom might be emotional, talk to your mom about it. Make sure you're expressing your emotions daily. You too should find ways that work best for you to manage your feelings. But at the end of the day, remember that it is a choice.

It's not your genetics causing you to respond the way that you do. You have complete control of your emotions. You always have and you always will. And just because you have the ability to control them, doesn't mean you're any good at it yet. Don't worry, we'll get into this more later too, but for now, I just want you to recognize that you have the power to control your emotions. You can't just blame your response mechanisms and your feelings on your genes.

Technology is a tool that you teens should use to the best of your ability, so make sure you use it for more than just games and social media. Dive into research if you want to better understand your emotions.

There are a zillion personality tests online that will assess your personality and help you to understand your emotions. Some personality tests will highlight your strengths and weaknesses and provide you with insight based on your fears and beliefs. It's fascinating how accurate some of these tests are too.

Exploring a personality test will help you to identify your individual personality and best understand your emotions. Then you can take it a step further and have members of your family take it too. You can all discuss your personalities and how they blend best together. I'm willing to bet you'll all have different personalities, which will prove my theory that you can't blame genetics! Knowing how everyone in your house responds to emotions will build awareness, trust, and acceptance between you and your family.

So, don't hold back. Dive into research and be productive about understanding your emotions. Find new ways to express yourself, but at the end of the day, stop bottling up your emotions. Now that you know you're in control, you know that the way you respond is a choice. Don't blame genetics.

More Tools in Your Toolbox

When you begin accepting your emotions and welcoming them with open arms, you develop new skills and increase your intelligence. I call this "adding more tools to your toolbox."

Embracing your emotions is going to help you for the rest of your life. Heck, it's something you can even add to your resume! When you reach a certain point in your teen years, maybe in a required class or a senior year presentation, you might have to create a resume to help prepare you for life after high school. You might even want to skip those classes and go straight to the part where you apply for your first job or internship.

When this day comes, you're going to need to bullet an array of honest characteristics about yourself. If you become a master at embracing your emotions, then you can write down any of these traits to boost your chances of getting the position you want:

- Has emotional agility
- Flexible and adaptable
- Resilient
- Persistent

- Malleable
- Understanding
- Empathizes with others
- Works well with others

All of those wonderful traits are an expression of having emotional capacity. If you learn to embrace your emotions, then you'll likely add any of those tools to your toolbox (and more too).

Give Yourself Grace

Embracing your emotions will become much easier if you learn to give yourself grace. I remember in high school, I would get so upset with myself over what now seems like the silliest things: if I scored low on a test, if I didn't wear the right outfit to school, or if I said the wrong thing when trying to comfort a friend. I was doing the best that I could, but I was still so hard on myself regardless of the situation.

Kid, if this sounds like you, then you need to listen up good. You need to stop doing this to yourself!

I made this mistake and I'm certain I walked down that path to make sure you don't have to.

If you make a silly mistake, it's totally OK! We need to learn to accept our mistakes and trust that we will learn from them. The mistakes that you've made in the past have gotten you to where you are today. You simply wouldn't be the same person without them.

Just think of when you get sick. Your body doesn't say, "Listen kid, you made a real mistake! You should never have caught a cold last weekend. Looks like we're shutting down!"

Um, how silly does that sound?

Like extremely silly…

Because it is.

When we get sick, our body's primal instinct is to immediately feel better again. Our white blood cells go to work to fight off those foreign invaders—and guess what! We don't even have to tell them to do it. It happens naturally. And a day later, we feel totally fine again! No more sniffles.

So compare that sickness to your common mistake and know that you're going to bounce right back from it.

Know that it's OK to make errors and for goodness' sake, stop torturing yourself for making them! Give yourself grace, my friends. It will make the process of embracing your emotions that much easier.

Emotional Contagion

Emotional contagion refers to the phenomenon of one person's emotions and behaviors directly triggering similar emotions and behaviors in other people.

Have you ever walked into your house with a smile on to find that someone else in the house had a bad day? Suddenly, their sour mood is causing a wave of negativity and you find yourself in a bad mood too. That's emotional contagion at its worst, but thankfully, it works in the opposite way as well.

Now think about a time when you came home after a bad day. (Maybe you peed yourself at school again.) Who knows, but just for fun, let's say you did pee yourself again! So now you've come home, you're in a bad mood and you just want to be left alone, but everyone in your house is so dang happy. Everyone is filled with smiles and laughter and positivity, and suddenly, you find yourself in a good mood. That's emotional contagion at its best.

I tell you this because it's a really powerful tool to know that your emotions are impacted by other people. Likewise, you have the power to impact those around you with your emotions as well.

I believe emotional contagion is the reason most of us tell people "to get back to a state of being happy." We fear that if someone around us is in a sour mood, then they're going to impact our mood and bring us into a state of negativity too. Thus, we encourage others to mask their feelings and pretend like everything's fine. Sometimes, we simply just don't know the right words to say either. That causes us to tell others to "feel better" and "be happy" and do things that a sad person doesn't necessarily feel like doing at the moment.

Understanding emotional contagion will help you to manage your emotions. And for that reason, we're going to do a little practice below. Remember, this book is a workbook, but it's all for you. No one is going to see the things you write down so be open, be honest, and use this book as a tool to help you manage your emotions.

Right now, I want you to write down in the box below every emotion you've felt in the last week. It might take you a few minutes to reflect on the last few days and that's fine. You have all the time you need. Just think: Were you happy? Sad? Angry? Disgusted? Surprised? Loving?

Embarrassed? Calm? Awkward? Bored? Comfortable? Uncomfortable? There's plenty of other emotions I could list but it's up to you! Write them down in the left column.

List of Emotions:

1.	
2.	
3.	
4.	
5.	
6.	
7.	
8.	
9.	
10.	

You wrote them all down? Great! Now write down in the right column why you were feeling that way. Who were you around? What happened that caused your emotion? Maybe you were feeling happy because you were with your friends. Maybe you were feeling sad because you couldn't spend time with friends. Whatever it is, write it down!

Once you're finished, look at everything you've listed. If there's a person, or people, in your life who are constantly filling you up with good vibes and happy emotions, then you should continue spending time with them. If there's a person, or people, in your life whose negative feelings tend to bring you to a state of unhappiness, then it's definitely something to be aware of. Try to spend less time around those people. If you can't, then awareness will be key in order to avoid catching the negative emotions you don't want to feel. Let's say maybe it's a classmate who you sit directly next to, or maybe it's someone that you live with. Regardless of the situation, if you can't avoid the person then at least you can be aware of it.

Being aware of your emotions is the most important part of managing them. When you know you're going to be in the presence of someone who tends to bring negative emotions, mentally prepare beforehand. There are plenty of ways you can mentally prepare and by reading the rest of this book and following the tips and strategies given, you'll be able to embrace emotional contagion and use it to your advantage.

Emotional Tip #1

Embrace your emotions and identify them. Keep a mood journal if you have to. This will look similar to the exercise you did in the chapter. Discover what emotions you feel and when they occur. How often do you experience these feelings? Who is around when you do? What environment are you in? Once you can identify them, you can move on to step number two.

Emotional Tip #2

Now that you can identify them, take a look at the impact your emotions have. Does the size of the situation match the size of your reaction? Will the problem matter in five years' time? If not, do you spend more than five minutes worrying with emotional overwhelmingness? Actively seek to manage your responses so that these two match. If the problem won't matter in five years' time, then don't spend more than five minutes stressing over it.

Emotional Tip #3

Practice self-care daily. When you're giving yourself the time, space, and rest that your body needs, it is much easier to manage your emotions. This is a very simple task, but often difficult to do. Learn how to say "no" to anything that doesn't raise your energy, your vibration, or your spirit. The more rest you get, the easier it will be to control your emotions. Self-care has become this cheesy thing that apparently you're only supposed to do on Sundays. That's not true, don't listen to it. If you want to have a healthy, vibrant life, then you need to practice self-care every dang day. Self-care is going to look different to everyone, it depends on what things you like to do. Some self-care activities that you might enjoy include: exercising; healthy nutrition; cooking; journaling; meditation; taking a walk through nature; drawing or painting; creating a list of goals; cleaning your house; attending therapy; reading a book; spending quality time with a loved one; and so on. For some of you, your favorite activities might not even be on that list. That's fine. It's personal to you, just make sure you schedule them into your day and label it a priority.

Emotional Tip #4

Avoid circumstances that trigger unwanted emotions. Too often, we embrace situations that we know cause overwhelming anxiety, anger, and stress to our emotional state. We'll get more into addictions in chapter 7, but it is possible to be addicted to chaos. I have known people who were and I'm sure you have too. Your teen years are often filled with chaos and drama, and sometimes, it might feel impossible to get away from. On the other hand, I'm here to tell you that it is possible. You need to learn how to avoid it instead of inviting it. If someone in your life is triggering for you, then avoid spending time with that person. If you get frustrated in your morning classes, then you might need to wake up earlier to feel more alert. In order to wake up earlier, you likely have to get to bed earlier. Don't watch television until midnight and then wake up grumpy because you didn't get enough rest. I'm not going to continue dragging this one out because I think you get the point. Plus, we'll talk more about sleep in chapter 4. Be proactive. Take charge of your life and control your emotions!

Emotional Tip #5

Complimenting people is the best way to avoid unwanted emotional contagion. If you focus on positive emotions and compliment everyone you interact with, you will create an upsurge of optimism and people will thrive off of you. Make your daily goal to make someone else's day better and you'll inevitably develop a domino effect of happiness to those around you. You'll likely refrain from catching other people's negative emotions just by being around them. If this doesn't work, compliment yourself. Do it in a cheesy way, I don't care. Say "Girl, I love your outfit" or "Man, you're really killin' it today!" Complimenting anyone, even yourself, has a way of avoiding unwanted emotional contagion.

Chapter 2
We All Want to Be Heard

Teddy Roosevelt is one of my favorite presidents. You'll see his name again in this book because I can't help but share some of his wisdom. In fact, this might be the best story ever and it's told by the 26th president himself.

During Roosevelt's presidency, he often endured long receiving lines where people would come up and shake his hand. It didn't take long for him to realize that people didn't do a good job of listening, even when it was the president speaking. So the day came where he decided to play a trick on his guests and test the theory whether people actually listened to the things that were being said to them.

As each guest arrived and shook Roosevelt's hand, he politely smiled and whispered, "I murdered my grandmother this morning."

I hope you laughed because I just about spit my water out when I first heard that. The best part of the story is that it went exactly how Roosevelt anticipated. Most people smiled back and said ridiculous things like "Marvelous!" or "How sweet!" or "God Bless You!"

It wasn't until the end of the line that one foreign diplomat actually listened to what he said. When the president whispered, "I murdered my grandmother this morning," the diplomat leaned in and responded, "I'm sure she had it coming."

Now I want you to learn two things from that story. One, President Roosevelt was pretty freaking hilarious. And two, the art of listening is dying.

Most of the time we're so distracted that we hear noise, or we see lips moving, but we don't actually process what other people are saying.

Think of the last time someone listened to what you had to say. And I mean *really* listened. They weren't texting on their phone or playing a video game or cooking dinner or any other type of distraction you can think of. They were sitting across from you, with great eye contact, and really listening to what you had to say.

Now think of how you felt afterwards. Did you feel better? Did you feel appreciated and like that person cared? Did you feel special and important enough that the person gave you quality time out of their day?

It's true that everyone likes to feel heard. We all like to feel listened to. That's something you'll never grow out of. Men, women, teens, old, young, it doesn't matter. Everyone wants to feel listened to. For as long as humans have existed, we thrive on comfort and the ability to communicate with one another. That's the sole way we have survived and developed into the civilized society we are today. It's our human instinct to be there for each other, to help each other, to connect, comfort, communicate, and listen to each other.

So, the question arises, do you have someone who will listen to you? You're at a pivotal point in your life where you teens (possibly more than any other age) are craving the attention and the desire for someone to listen to you. You want someone to hear your stories, both good and bad. You want someone to hear your feelings, your thoughts, your dreams, your fears, your wild weekends, your outfit choice for the football game, and your thoughts about homecoming.

It's not good enough that you want someone to listen to you, but heck, I'll go as far as saying you *need* someone to listen to you. Being heard is one of the best ways to express your emotions and build connections with others. You develop the skill sets to be a great communicator while also reflecting on your own experiences. Conversation is a wonderful thing.

So, back to that question, do you have someone who will listen to you?

If the answer is no, then it's time you find someone. It can be a friend, a parent, a sibling, a cousin, a grandparent, a teacher, a neighbor, a mentor, a therapist, it doesn't matter who it is. But tell that person you admire them (I'm sure they'll appreciate it!) and ask if they'd be willing to listen to you talk. Carve time in your day that works for you both (as I'm sure you're both busy) but it's important that you feel heard. If you haven't experienced this yet in your life, then I promise you it's worth a try. Being listened to is a wonderful revelation and it's something we all crave on a daily basis, especially when you're a teenager.

Practice Listening to Other People Too

Interrupting someone while talking is often someone's way of keeping the conversation moving. People even think by interrupting with their own points that they are adding valuable content. This, however, is an extremely ineffective way to communicate. In fact, it might possibly be the worst thing you could do. The highest form of listening is letting other people communicate their ideas and finish their sentences.

With that being said, I want you to pause right now and think of how often you do this. And be truthful, you guys! The only person you're opening up to is yourself.

The reason I want you to do this is because most people tend to interrupt others when they're talking. Most people jump in with their ideas because they want to sound smart and relatable. Most people think, *If I don't comment right now then I'm not going to remember my comment later.* So we jump in and interrupt the person who's talking. That shows the other person you're done listening to them and you have something more important to say. It shows that you don't really care to hear the rest of their thoughts. It implies that you aren't really listening to the best of your ability.

Now think of how annoying that is when it happens to you. Imagine coming home after a long day of school, telling your mom a story that's been on your mind all day, and she interrupts you to try to guess the details of the story. Your mom acts as if she already knows what happened. She responds by saying the exact same thing has happened to her and now the story is all about her experience and not yours.

How freaking annoying is that!

If you're guilty of this, which by gosh, I'm sure you are, then it's time to start focusing on becoming a better listener. And trust me, you are not alone in this, my friend. Even adults are still practicing this skill. So, wouldn't it be amazing if you got ahead of the game now? You could perfect this skill long before your adult years and help others to do it too!

When we switch the conversation and take the spotlight away from the storyteller, it signifies that you don't care about their story. The best solution would be to wait until the end. Don't interrupt. Let them share all the details they have to spill. People love talking about themselves so let them do it! Allow other people to lead the conversation while you practice the art of listening. When they are done, then you can respond with a relatable comment. You can say, "Wow, that's so interesting! I can totally understand why you feel that way…"

Along with interrupting, people often tend to finish other people's sentences. TV sitcoms like to show this as a cute thing that friends or significant others do because they know each other so well. Unfortunately, this was a lie that I was taught at a very young age, possibly even before high school. I thought if I could finish someone's sentence, then it would affirm my listening skills and show them that I understand.

This was entirely wrong and I hope you teens will do a better job of this than I did.

When you try to finish someone else's sentence, then you steal control of the conversation. If someone's looking for a specific word to use then don't jump in and suggest a word for them. If you do, then you're implying that you're in a hurry to end the conversation. It might even suggest that you think your words are better. Be patient and let other people finish their sentences. Let them find their own words.

When I was in high school, I labeled myself as a good listener. In fact, my whole life I'd labeled myself a good listener. I thought I listened to people when they talked, paid attention, and showed sincere interest in my responses. Learning these simple flaws in my communication skills made me extremely uncomfortable. It made me realize I had a lot of work to do.

So, kid, if that's you too, then it's OK.

If you're uncomfortable reading this because you know you have a lot of work to do, then let's dive in and do it together. Remember, you're not alone in this. It's like learning to ride a bike. It might take you a few tries, but I promise, you'll get the hang of it.

Developing the skills to be a good listener will be an amazing revelation for you. It'll be "another tool for your toolbox" as you know I'd like to say. (Don't laugh at me, I know I'm cheesy!)

For one, the pressure will be off you. You'll no longer feel pressure to say the right thing. By letting others talk and say what they have to say, you'll never have to find the perfect words. If you simply focus on listening, then you don't have to worry about your own personal response— only theirs.

Have you ever been in a conversation with someone and three seconds—no joke—three seconds after you said something, you thought to yourself, *Why did I just say that?*

Well, I can tell you that has happened to me hundreds of times. Probably even thousands if I reflect back to high school. The reason I was so guilty of this is because I would jump in and respond to someone at a point where it wasn't necessary.

Silence is sometimes the loudest response. Silence can suggest understanding, sympathy, empathy, faith, acceptance, sorrow, fear, anger, disappointment, and so many other emotions.

I no longer regret saying something or feel embarrassed for saying the wrong thing.

There are plenty of things you could do to work on becoming a better listener. Minimize your distractions and keep eye contact. Practice the beautiful art of listening.

Listen to Learn

U.S. History is one of my favorite subjects. It's so fun learning about how much we've grown in the last 245 years. As far as countries go, we're basically a baby compared to some other nations and we've been through an incredible amount of things. Between the American Revolution and today, we've endured dozens of awesome time periods including some of my favorites: the Gilded Age, the Progressive Era, and the Roaring Twenties.

Understanding history is a treasure that opens you up to another time period. It's like getting in a time machine and seeing what life looked like decades before you were even born. History is pretty stinkin' cool.

Unfortunately for my teenage self, I didn't understand the art of listening and I certainly didn't listen to learn. Thus, it might be hard for you to believe but my history grades actually suffered in high school. I'm not kidding either, they really suffered. But it's not because I didn't enjoy the subject. It's simply because I didn't listen to learn.

Throughout most of my time in high school, I listened to people out of generosity rather than out of pure interest in what they had to say. It wasn't until many years later that I realized people are gifts and when they speak, it's valuable information that I want to soak up.

My advice to you teens is to start looking at people as if they're a book that you've never read before. Each person has multiple chapters in their book and there's so much content you have to learn. All you have to do is read the book, or in other words, listen to what they have to say.

Brendan Cartlidge, M.Ed., my brother-in-law, and one of the coolest guys I know, says, "Listening is less about the words and more about the feeling. One must listen with their whole self, their eyes, their ears, their heart, and soul to truly hear."

When you start listening with the intention of learning something new, your presence in each conversation will change dramatically. If you change your mindset, this could be a whole new tool in your toolbox.

Listening Tip #1

Stop talking so much! Seriously, guys, take a second and think about your conversations. Are you the one who does the most talking? Are your conversations 50/50 or does one person typically control the conversation? If you are doing the majority of the talking, then you might not be doing a great job listening to those around you. Great conversations occur when it's a 50/50 split or when the other person does more talking than you. You might be asking "why do I want to hear someone else talk more than me?" and don't worry, you're not alone in this. I would definitely insert a laughing emoji here if I could, because I used to feel that way too. It wasn't until recently that I realized when I'm doing the talking, I'm only sharing information that I already know. If I do less talking and more listening, then I soak up more information and learn from those who are talking. Secondly, as I mentioned earlier, the pressure is off when I'm the one listening. I no longer have to worry about having the perfect response. So ask yourself this question: what are the ratios of my conversations?

Listening Tip #2

Observe the moments when you're not truly listening to someone. I'm sure you all know someone whose best quality is their ability to talk. Maybe it's a friend or a parent or a sibling. Whoever it is, they're likely a social butterfly who loves to talk and talk and talk. If that's the case, I'm sure there have been moments when you weren't really listening. You might be thinking about something else that you felt was more important at that moment. If this is true for you, you're prioritizing your thoughts over the person who's talking. There might be times when you can be honest with that person and tell them that you're distracted by something else. And there will be other times where you can practice changing that habit. In order to stay focused on the person talking, ask questions throughout the conversation. This will hold you accountable to make sure you're actively listening to the speaker. It'll keep you engaged and more interested in what they are saying. If you find yourself not truly listening to someone while they're speaking or drifting off thinking about something else in your mind, then reconsider your priorities. Make others your priority and acknowledge the importance of learning from them.

Listening Tip #3

When in a conversation, make sure to always respond at the other person's level. OK, OK, some of you might be confused by this so let me break it down for you. When listening to someone speak, they're not only telling you words but they're also communicating their emotions. When you respond, make sure to meet their emotions. If someone is upset, don't respond with a loud, happy tone. Doing this would likely make someone uncomfortable. If someone is super excited and pumped about a college acceptance, don't respond with a bitter, melancholy tone. That would also make someone uncomfortable. In addition to their emotions, look for comfort words. If someone is speaking and you notice a specific word they've used multiple times, then make sure to use that word too. My infamous brother-in-law and Admissions Consultant Brendan Cartlidge loves storytelling and always says "In any event." So whenever it's my turn to tell a story, I make sure to use his catch phrase and intentionally build our connection.

Listening Tip #4

Empathize with their point-of-view. There's nothing I dislike more than an intense, combative political conversation. In fact, I don't like any type of confrontation so I'd always prefer to avoid conflict. That's why this tip is my favorite. When someone is speaking, acknowledge their point-of-view. Do you agree with them or disagree with them? Honestly, the answer doesn't matter because you can still engage in great, positive, friendly conversation when you disagree with someone. Make sure to listen to the details, hear their perspective, and empathize with their point-of-view. Doing this will undoubtedly build your connection with those around you.

Listening Tip #5

Stop listening out of generosity and hear what other people are trying to say to you. Make it a goal to learn one new fact in every conversation and you will start appreciating your conversations much more. You won't simply be listening out of courtesy, but instead, you'll be listening to learn.

Chapter 3
Anxiety Is Normal

According to the National Institute of Health, one in three teens living in the United States today will experience an anxiety disorder.

Did you read that?

One in three teens.

That number blew my mind when I first read that. That's like 33.333333% of all teens! (I passed Math, I swear!)

The reason it blew my mind was not because I felt like the number was high, but actually I felt like the number was low.

Shouldn't all teens have anxiety? Shouldn't all *people* have anxiety?

Anxiety is defined as a feeling of worry, nervousness, or unease, typically about an imminent event or something with an uncertain outcome.

Well, when I read that definition, it sounded an awful lot like the definition of worrying, which is defined as giving way to anxiety or unease; allowing one's mind to dwell on difficulty or troubles.

You: *So, anxiety is basically an extreme case of worrying?*

Basically. Yes. It's a debilitating feeling of restlessness, panic, impending doom, danger, and fear, with goosebumps and sweaty palms all wrapped up into one. It can be pretty freaking awful in extreme phases.

I would never want to downplay anxiety because I know it's a real thing that millions and millions of people are dealing with today. Especially teens. But when I realized that anxiety is the concept of worrying too much, I felt like it should be a healthy emotion. Isn't worrying a normal, healthy human emotion? The answer is yes. It *should* be a healthy emotion, but when people experience disproportionate levels of anxiety, it becomes a medical disorder that doctors can even prescribe medications for.

You: But Nicole, doesn't everyone feel the emotion of worrying?

Well, I thought so too. Everyone experiences the feeling of being worrisome. I can imagine cavemen who walked the Earth 2.5 million years ago felt constant anxiety about whether they were going to live or die. Would they get eaten by the end of the day? Would they be ridden of disease or find enough food to last them the week? I'm sure they had so many things to worry about and yet, none of them were diagnosed with an anxiety disorder.

Let's take a brief look at history here. According to the American Psychiatric Association, generalized anxiety disorder was first discovered in 1980. Prior to that, the term "anxiety neurosis" was used, and it was first mentioned in 1895 by Austrian neurologist Sigmund Freud. Then, before that, it was much, much more uncommon to come across than it is today.

It's not that it didn't exist, it just wasn't as widely talked about and honestly, we didn't really know what it was. But that doesn't mean people didn't feel anxious about the future. Of course, they did. Because just like we are now, people were uncertain about what the future would hold. It's arguable that we're actually living in the most certain times that mankind has ever seen. Why? Well, the answer is easy. We know that the world is round with seven continents and billions of people. We have the tools, the knowledge, the power to access resources like we've never been able to access before. We've advanced so much as a human species that we've even been able to build a rocket and launch humans off into space! How freaking crazy is that? So, like I said, it's arguable that we're living in the most certain times that mankind has ever endured.

With that said, I'm sure millions of people throughout history have experienced anxiety. Think about the families whose loved ones went overseas to war and the families who lived during the Great Depression, unsure of what the following day would bring. Think of the Spanish flu and how we were so unsure of the virus that some scientists believed it was an adverse *influence* of the stars or an alignment of the planets. Hence the name *influenza* because it was originally coined *influentia* or *influence* in medieval Latin. (I had to add this in here because it's one of my favorite stories!)

Thank goodness we learned enough in the last century to know the Coronavirus was a global pandemic and not the alignment of the planets influencing us. Can you imagine how crazy that would sound? It's wild to think about how much we've learned since the start of mankind, and I know we're going to continue learning more and more each day.

Now kid, let's go back to my initial comment about that statistic that states only 33% of teens experience anxiety. I didn't like that number when I first read it and I still don't like it now. I think 100% of teens experience anxiety, and the fact that we're creating a statistic that labels the teens who openly express their feelings doesn't sit right with me.

What I'm about to say is truthfully how I feel in my gut and I hope you believe it too. I want you to read these words and I hope they stick with you for the rest of your life: anxiety is normal.

It's totally normal. It's a part of our genetic make-up. Everyone experiences bouts of anxiety. We're human beings and we experience plenty of emotions, some that make us comfortable and some that make us uncomfortable. Anxiety just so happens to be one of those extremely uncomfortable feelings and it sucks but it's normal.

If you are someone who experiences anxiety, and if you are diagnosed with an anxiety disorder because you experience it in extreme amounts, then trust me when I say this, but you are totally normal. There's nothing wrong with you and you're going to make it through this. I told you a little bit of history because I want you to know that anxiety isn't a new feeling and you're not alone. People have been experiencing anxiety for thousands of years and people will continue to feel this emotion for thousands of years to come.

It can be a terrible feeling, I know. It makes you extremely uncomfortable, I know. But guess what else?

I truly believe getting out of your comfort zone and doing things that make you uncomfortable is the best possible way to experience growth. So, if you experience anxiety, then I say you're ahead of the game.

I think it's time to change the narrative attached to anxiety. I say we stop letting this crippling worrying emotion bring us to our knees. Teens who are struggling with anxiety should embrace this challenge and know that it's not going to be the end of you. It's only the beginning. They say that what doesn't kill you makes you stronger, and experiencing bouts of anxiety is going to make you that much stronger on the other side. So it's time to take the bull by the horns and embrace it.

A Blessing in Disguise

Now that you've learned that anxiety is normal and that you should embrace your emotions, let's talk about how it's actually a blessing in disguise.

You might be thinking, *Nicole, there's no way my anxiety is a blessing,* and I totally understand why you might think that. But I tend to think it is. In fact, most of our biggest challenges *are* blessings in disguise. It's divine nature telling you that an unfortunate event actually has meaningful results in the end.

Don't believe me? Let's look at some examples:

Let's say you're going through your first break-up. It's the first time you've ever experienced heartache and it's painful and confusing, but it signifies that person wasn't who you're meant to be with. Eventually, you will find your soulmate and be happy with the end results.

Or we could look at another example. Let's say you missed the bus to school today and your morning hasn't been going well. What seems like a bad start to the day is actually a blessing in disguise because now your mom is driving you to school and you can stop at Dunkin Doughnuts for breakfast. (Definitely a blessing in my book!)

And lastly, we can look at one more example. Let's say you're in the 33% of teens who are struggling with anxiety. It often interferes with your day and it seems like a major roadblock to you, something holding you back from living life to your fullest potential. So you begin researching coping mechanisms and you develop a passion for psychology. Little did you know that your experience with anxiety would lead to your career choice later in life.

Ultimately, life is everything that we make it to be. When challenges come knocking at your door, don't let them take over your life. Challenges are here to make you stronger so view them as opportunities. Ask yourself these questions: How do you normally respond to daily situations? Do you feel like good things are always happening to you or does it seem like bad things are always happening? Are you the type that looks at the glass half full or half empty?

I've mentioned this before and I'll say it again. Challenges are inevitable. They will come and go throughout your entire life so it's critical to start viewing them as opportunities for growth. Stop telling yourself that bad situations are always happening to you and start breathing life into those challenges. If you can, shift your beliefs to think that these situations are positively happening *for* you, then I promise you, kid, you're going to start feeling a lot happier. Sometimes, it can be hard to find meaning in something bad that happened, but if you give it enough time, patience, and room for growth, I'm sure you'll find a meaning for it.

Think about this too: How boring would our lives be if everything always worked out perfectly? I can't even begin to tell you how *boring* that sounds! Accept the challenges and let them mold you into a better, smarter, stronger version of yourself. When life gives you lemons, don't just make lemonade. Open up a whole dang lemonade stand and make a drink for everyone!

It's Time You Clean Out Your Closet

When I was in high school, I had so many clothes it was insane. I loved having a different outfit for every occasion and even when I stopped wearing certain clothes, I could never let them go. I probably had three dozen hoodies of my hometown athletic apparel. I had heels that I would never wear, cleats, sneakers, sandals, slippers, boots, and every type of jewelry you could imagine. I had sweaters and jeans and shirts and dresses, and I probably had all of these things x10. I had clothes overflowing from my own closet, and I raided the closet in our hallway, our guest room, and I even had boxes of clothes stacked in our attic.

Needless to say, I'm fairly confident I had a hoarding disorder. In fact, over 19 million Americans *do* have a hoarding disorder and it's more common than you'd think. It sounds crazy but I even felt a sense of pride, feeling great about the fact that I'd hoarded a bunch of junk for years. Seriously, there was a point in my life where I'm pretty sure

I could have had my own episode on *True Life. I Am a Hoarder* edition.

Well, I don't think it was a coincidence that at times I felt cluttered, stressed, or anxious.

Research shows that excess clutter is associated with life dissatisfaction. Clutter negatively impacts our mental wellbeing, and particularly in women, it induces a psychological response that increases cortisol, a stress hormone.

I always knew that I loved a clean space and an organized environment, but until researching, I never knew why. This was very enlightening to me, and as I grew older, I became passionate about getting rid of all the unnecessary junk from my closet and I only wish I knew this in my teen years.

Decluttering is a part of minimalism, which focuses on more time and more mental space. Clutter attacks our mind with excessive stimuli, causing our senses to work overtime on things that aren't truly necessary. Clutter distracts us, drawing our attention away from what's really important in life. Having less stuff to clean, organize, and look at leads to being more present with friends and family.

At first, I was skeptical, but it seemed worth a try.

I raided my own closet and threw out about 90% of what was in it. It was an intense afternoon, I'll admit, but the happiness I felt when throwing all this junk out was unlike any other. Not only had I been holding onto most of these clothes for years, but they were holding onto specific emotions too.

A pair of jeans I could no longer fit into, but I kept telling myself one day I would. It made me feel like I wasn't working hard enough.

A sleeveless top that I didn't feel comfortable wearing because my skin wasn't clear enough. There was no hiding it and it made me feel self-conscious.

A few dresses from Mexico that I never wore because they were three times my size. I felt obligated to hold onto them because my parents gifted them to me. I also felt guilty for not once wearing them.

A sparkly pair of heels that I once wore to a homecoming dance. It reminded me of the guy I dated and didn't want to think about anymore.

It was insane.

Who would've thought the clothes in our closet could trigger negative responses? Kid, if you haven't done this in your life, then it is imperative. You *need* to go through your closet and get rid of the clothes that aren't serving you. I promise this will boost your energy and make you happier, which in turn, will change your entire life.

If you're someone struggling with anxiety and have been for years, I encourage you to take a good look at your surroundings. Is your private space filled with junk or do you have a clean, open space to depress and unwind?

My sister has been talking about tiny-homes since we were in high school. She would always send me pictures of tiny houses on wheels and say, "This is my future home!"

"But what about having privacy?" I would ask, curiously. "And could your friends come sleep over? Does it have to be on wheels?"

She would always giggle and say, "It's all I need!"

And I would politely nod and stop asking a dozen questions, but deep down I thought she was a crazy person.

My sister, wise beyond her years and a self-proclaimed minimalist, was right. She knew the significance of clearing the clutter and clearing the mind.

Connecting with Others Who Also Might Have Anxiety

I've said this a few times already, but let's take a look at that statistic one last time. Today, one in three teens living in the United States will experience an anxiety disorder.

That means when you look amongst your peers, it's likely that some of your friends are experiencing the same fears and stressors that you are. I love that for two reasons. One, it's a gentle reminder that you're never alone. Millions of other kids (and adults too for that matter) are experiencing the same things as you. While you are unique and authentic in your own skin, you're also never, ever alone. The second reason I love it is because if you know that your peers are experiencing feelings of overwhelm, stress, or worry, then wouldn't you want to help them?

I know I sure would!

And it's definitely possible to do so! I'm going to give you some tips on how you can help your peers embrace their feelings of anxiety, while also helping your own.

A couple of years ago, the phrase "being present in the moment" became really popular and lately, it's something that everyone's been talking about. There is meaning behind it though.

It has everything to do with your awareness. Are you attentive during your day-to-day activities or do you find yourself going through the motions? Do you constantly feel like life is a battle and negative things happen to you? Or do you wake up daily with the reminder that life is a blessing and there is meaning in everything that happens?

Maybe you've never thought of those questions before and you don't even have an answer to them. Regardless of where you stand, it's something we need to talk more about.

Being present in the moment helps you to appreciate the moment as it's happening. For example, right now, I'm writing this chapter while sitting on the couch and my echo dot is playing music in the background. At this moment, I'm present and aware that this moment will come to an end. This day will eventually come to an end, as will this year, and this chapter of the book. I reflect back on my high school days and wish I had spent more time living in the present moment. I was often focused on the past or on the future, two places that I physically wasn't able to be in.

I've learned to appreciate the days because now I know in a very short period of time I'm going to miss this moment—the one that I'm in right now.

When you're present, you're aware of your surroundings and you feel grateful for the moment that you're in. When you develop a practice of gratitude, you begin to glow.

The definition of glowing means to show strong and happy emotions. Now just think, if you intentionally show strong, happy emotions at various times throughout the day, wouldn't you be an overall jovial person? I can guarantee you that your peers would start to see your glowingness and want more of it. People will gravitate toward you, they'll want to be around you, and your energy will be contagious.

Now, let's do a full review to wrap this up. We talked about actively being more present in the moment. When you do, you'll feel grateful for the times you're currently in. You won't feel anxious thinking about things that might happen in the future and you won't feel stressed or embarrassed about things that may have happened yesterday. It is nearly impossible to feel anxiety and gratitude simultaneously. Thus, your gratitude will result in a euphoric sense of freedom. You'll feel free from anxiety and open to happier, blissful emotions. Your peers will sense this excitement and the positive energy that's glowing off of you. They'll want more of your energy, and then you can teach them exactly how you got it.

It's so simple that it's genius. And what's even more exciting is that it's all up to you! This new and improved lifestyle shift is at your fingertips. You just need to start.

Anxiety Tip #1

Learning how to say "no" when you don't really want to do something is one of the best things you can do to control your anxiety. You'll never feel stressed awaiting events that you don't want to attend or doing things that you don't want to do. One of my peloton icons, Robin Arzon who cheers me on while I run, mentioned this quote: "If it doesn't raise my energy, my vibration, my spirit, or my bank account, then the answer is no!" That quote resonated with me so well and I swear I live by those words. I wanted to share it with you in hopes that it resonates with you too.

The word "no" is critical to my growth, controlling my emotions, and preventing quick, angry responses. It's imperative for you to be able to say "no" in order to show up as the teen you want to be to your family, your friends, your teachers, and to the rest of the world.

Anxiety Tip #2

Do three things for yourself daily. The more time you spend focusing on yourself in the moment, the less time you spend anxiously awaiting future events. When I discovered this magical skill of not worrying about things that haven't even happened yet, I had more time to do the things that I love. And when I do the things that make me feel good, I'm a more positive, energetic, happier version of me. Everything just works better. Now, I make it a point to do three things for myself daily and I think as a teen, doing three things for yourself could really come in handy. Those three things may change but on average they may look like any of these: running, biking, reading, writing, practicing gratitude, being outside, taking a yoga class, swimming, having a picnic, etc. Your list might look different than mine and that's perfectly fine! It should look different. Do the things that light *your* soul on fire and kick those horrible anxiety jitters to the curb.

Anxiety Tip #3

I already mentioned this in chapter 1, but this is so important that it's worth saying again. Avoid circumstances that trigger unwanted emotions. Too often we embrace situations that we know cause overwhelming anxiety, anger, and stress to our emotional state. Is it possible that you have an addiction to chaos? Do you look for anxiety-inducing activities? Be honest with yourself too. It's OK if the answer is yes, because I used to be there too. When I was a teen, the answer absolutely would have been yes. Even though it seems easy enough, it can be an enlightening tip for you. Stop following chaos around and avoid circumstances that trigger unwanted emotions. If you do, you will likely notice your anxiety levels decrease.

Anxiety Tip #4

Limit your social media use daily. Technology is here to stay and we are completely consumed with it. You might get annoyed with your parents when they limit your technology time, but I promise it's necessary. Adults need to limit their technology time too so you're not alone either. We all do. Research proves that social media causes depression and anxiety because it tricks your mind into staying up late, it impacts your ability to sleep, it allows you to view other peoples' highlight reels, you constantly compare yourself to other people, and so many other anxiety-inducing behaviors. Limit your time on it and you'll see immediate results. You'll stop judging, stop comparing, and you'll be able to focus on you alone.

Anxiety Tip #5

Minimizing will be a game-changer. I can't stress this one enough. Probably because it was so much fun to me, though I understand some of you may not find cleaning as enjoyable. I'm a fairly clean person to begin with and when

I was a teen, I still had way too much junk overflowing in my life. Minimalizing my room, my closet, and all excess spaces was such an exhilarating process and removed the unnecessary distractions that weren't serving me. I'll say it again if you didn't hear me the first dozen times: minimalize, minimalize, minimalize! Your anxiety will likely decline.

Anxiety Tip #6

Get your daily exercise in. This is going to lead me to the next chapter, so I promise I'll go into more detail then, but I truly believe you cannot feel anxiety and activity simultaneously. No matter what kind of exercising you do, if you get your heartbeat up enough, then you're going to decrease the amount of anxiety you feel on a daily basis. So get outside, get in the sun, exercise for at least 30 minutes per day, and eat a balanced nutritional diet. This leads me to our next topic.

Chapter 4
Make Your Health a Priority

You may have just rolled your eyes at the title of this chapter because it probably seems like a no-brainer by now. Everyone preaches the importance of health and how you need to do a better job maintaining it.

But here's what blows my mind. As obvious as it may seem, I don't think our school systems do a great job teaching us what we need to know about our health. At least they didn't when I was in high school. I remember hearing "Don't do drugs" and "Don't get STDs" in Health and Sex Ed., but I certainly don't remember learning about proper nutrition and how food impacts my body. I don't remember learning about the significance of sleep and how your body releases hormones throughout the day for optimal sleep and creativity times. I don't remember learning that the healthy amount of water intake per day is half a person's body weight (in oz). I don't remember learning about vitamins and nutrients and how there are proper proportions of each we should take daily.

What I do remember is watching celebrities advertise products on TV and everyone's goal was to look like that famous person. (Hello, Jennifer Anniston and Aveeno skin care!) But the sad thing was that nobody seemed to care about what ingredients were actually in the products we were using. Where is the class that teaches us how to read labels? And how to understand what we're putting into our bodies?

Disclaimer: there was none.

I hope I don't offend anyone here, but I truly think we really need to make some changes in our school systems. Teens today are growing up with access to so much information but aren't getting the tools or education they need in order to process the information and use it to their advantage.

Thus, this chapter is dedicated to making your health a priority. I know you understand that health is important, but have you ever asked yourself *why*? Do you know what things will impact you in the short term or long term? It's not about cutting calories or trying to look good in a sports outfit. It's about a balanced nutritional diet and moving your body. It's about optimal sleep times and getting sunlight during the day. Some of those might even sound basic but we're going to go into the details of each and break them down, because I think if every teen actually understood the reasonings behind *why* these things are so critical, then you'd all be striving to do them.

Movement Is Medicine

The mind and the body are inherently connected. Just think about it. When you feel nervous, your stomach gets jittery. When you feel depressed, you lose your appetite. When you feel stressed, your muscles tense up, and so on.

In order for your mind to be strong, your body needs to be strong. Movement is medicine. Movement is therapy. If you are feeling anxious, it's likely because you are stagnant.

Movement strengthens the mind and helps you think clearly. It's the ability to complete tasks efficiently and simply do more throughout the day.

Our bodies are much like a machine and we require basic necessities in order to function. Movement is one of those necessities. Outside of the mind, when you move your body, you strengthen the muscles, which ultimately improves stability, balance, and coordination. Movement helps the circulation in your body. It allows things to continue working as they should, to release hormones at certain times of the day, to metabolize, digest, and boost your immunity. Fitness makes you think better, feel better, perform better in all aspects of life.

When I was in high school, I didn't have the healthiest digestion and I was uncomfortable with my body. I was overweight and didn't understand why because I ate the same amount of food that most of my friends did. I always struggled with the bathroom and I didn't go regularly (sorry if that's TMI!). I saw doctors and experts in their field who told me there's nothing wrong and I should be going to the bathroom. None of them ever asked me "Do you move your body?" or "Do you drink enough water?" or "Do you consume fruits and vegetables every day?" If they had, then it would have solved many issues for me early on, but unfortunately, they didn't.

Everything in your body requires you to move. Everything in your body requires water. It wasn't until my late teen years, after graduating high school, that I began researching the significance of health and how your body functions. When I did, I was able to solve my own digestion issues. I lost the extra weight that was sitting on my midsection, but not because I wanted to look a certain way, I wanted to feel a certain way. When everything in your body is running smoothly the way it should, your body naturally sheds excess weight from proper metabolism. On top of all of this, I got my confidence back.

I've never been the type of person to step on a scale and stare at the numbers. I don't think you should be either and I hope you aren't. With that said, I wasn't staring at the scale hoping to lose weight. But I know that I did because my digestive system started working and I could literally see my body getting healthier day by day. My skin cleared up too (that was huge!) and it was all from learning to move my body and eat the right foods.

When you feel healthy, you feel confident. If confidence is something you lack, then do me a favor. Put this book down right now and vow to move your body. If the sun is out, go outside and go for a walk or a jog or a bike ride, or whatever it is that you like to do outside. If it's night time, then get on the floor and do some stretching. It doesn't have to be an overly strenuous activity. Stretching is still movement, and it helps to maintain your muscle health and strengthen your bones.

Nutrition Is Key

Alongside movement, nutrition is vital to making sure everything in your body is functioning the way that it should be. This too played a big role in having a healthy digestive system and clearing up my skin. Unfortunately though, when I was younger and I saw the food pyramid, it appeared to me that you're supposed to eat a large amount of grains per day. I thought that was the healthy thing to do.

In addition to that twist of the mind, I was also raised in a family with two full-time working parents. They worked hard during the day and didn't want to come home and fight with their children over eating their vegetables. I totally don't blame them for it either. It was definitely easier that way, and allowing me to eat grilled cheese and bread rolls made me momentarily happy too, so at the time it wasn't a bad gig. But unfortunately, my palette was born at a young age. I ate a ton of bread and a ton of dairy, and when I quickly grew into an overweight adolescent, I didn't understand what I was doing wrong.

Having access to this knowledge will be amazing for you teens because you can simply go online and research dozens of ways to eat healthier. There's a million resources for you too, which is great, but it can also make it tricky. With so many options, it might be hard to pick which one is right for you. So I'm going to give you some fun facts about nutrition that will arm you with the knowledge to make the right decisions for your health.

One of the most impactful changes I made to my diet was cutting back on gluten. It is said that over 50% of our population has a sensitivity to gluten and we don't even know it. Why don't we know it? Because we're not taught the signs and the symptoms for us to even realize. When you eat bread, do you tend to feel bloated? Do you ever get cramps? Or acne? Or headaches? Or feel lethargic? Or constipated? Any of these symptoms could be a direct result from eating gluten. If any of those stick out to you, then try cutting back on gluten for a few days. See if it makes a difference. If it does, then make a change in your life to consume a little less gluten. I'm not saying cut it out forever, but make the healthy choice to cut back on it. I know from experience that kids today are growing up eating way too much bread. It's not your fault, it's just the truth, and it could be detrimental to your health.

I know most kids are picky eaters, but if you're willing to dabble around and find the best nutritional options for you then I highly recommend doing so. Why? The answer is simple. Because even though your whole life people have been telling you how to eat, and what to eat, it's not as simple as that. Every single person on Earth is unique and everyone's diets are going to be slightly different. So try different things. Eliminate common allergens for a few days to see if they are right for you. If they don't, then add them back in. Be open to change, new foods, and eat a variety of colors because the more variety you consume, the more variety of nutrients you'll absorb. Learn from me and don't just stick to bread and cheese during all your teen years.

Another thing you might want to ask yourself is how much water do I drink per day? I mentioned this in the beginning of the chapter, but it's so significant that I want to bring it up again. This was definitely not something I was taught at a young age, and being an athlete my whole life, I can't believe no one ever told me sooner! We're supposed to drink half our body weight in water (in oz of course!) every single day. So let's use the number 100 (just because it's easy math for my brain). If someone weighs 100 pounds, then that person should be drinking at least 50oz of water every day. If it's 200 pounds, then 100 oz. Get it? It's simple math.

Kid, if there is anything outside of moving your body that I want you to learn here, then it's this. Make sure you're drinking enough water every day. Without it, we physically can't function. Get yourself a 32oz water bottle and make sure you refill it 2, 3, 4, 5 times per day, pending on how much you need to consume. Your body will thank you.

Sunlight Is Your Best Friend

Many of us are so cooped up indoors that we don't realize we're actually lacking exposure to sunlight. Adults and teens alike. We spend the majority of our days inside the comfort of our home and often in front of some type of screen; be it a computer, a phone, a tablet, a television, etc. Even when we leave our homes and go to school or work, we commute to another *indoor* location. Sometimes, on a sunny day, we might feel like we've gotten sunlight because our blinds are pulled up and rays of sunshine are beaming into the building, but unfortunately, those beams are not enough. That isn't the direct sunlight we need and when the day is done, most of us haven't spent any time outside basking in real, natural light.

Unfortunately, that lack of exposure is doing more than just keeping us from a nice tan, but it's depriving us from proper nutrient intake that we naturally get from the sun. We all know that flowers need natural light to grow and we humans are pretty much the same way. *We physically need it.* The sun provides us with vitamin D and wards off seasonal depression.

Being indoors messes with our circadian clock and causes us to stay up late and sleep less. Research shows that increased sunlight exposure will result in a better night's sleep. Think about a time when you spent hours outside, whether it be a birthday party or a family barbecue. I bet that night you slept like you did when you were a baby. That's because the sun physically wears you out and helps you to fall asleep naturally. It sounds a little crazy, and maybe even contradictory, that massive amounts of sunlight during the day can help you sleep better at night, but as you've probably learned in school, science doesn't lie. It's the truth and the research is out there.

It's Time to Get Some Sleep

I feel like there are two types of teenagers in the world. The ones who say "we'll sleep when we're dead" because they want to spend as much time as possible with their friends before graduation. They stay up late playing games, or sometimes they stay out late, and probably get nagged by their parents to come home and get some sleep. (I'll totally be that parent too, so don't hate on them!)

Secondly, there are the teens who love to sleep more than they love ice cream and they try to sleep as much as possible. Regardless of where you stand, there's more to sleeping than we're taught in school and I'm here to fill you in on the details.

When it comes to making your health a priority, sleep doesn't often come up as the main topic of discussion. It's extremely overlooked and outside of your doctor telling you to get 8 hours, there's not much information teens have on it. So why is sleep so important and how does it impact us?

Research has proven that the brain doesn't stop developing until the age of 25. So, during your teenage years, you're arguably in the most important stage of your life because how you treat your body now could impact you for the rest of your life. It is said that teens should sleep between 8 and 10 hours per night. Giving yourself plenty of rest will help your body to grow physically, mentally, and emotionally. Your body will be able to recover and restore the parts of your body that have been fully active in the hours that you were awake.

If you need a good example to understand the role of sleep in the development process, then just think of a baby. Maybe you have a younger sibling or a cousin that you watched grow up. Or maybe you have a friend with a younger sibling. Regardless of how you know them, I'm willing to bet that the baby sleeps several hours a day. I'm sure that the baby takes multiple naps throughout the day and sleeps long hours at night. And you know what? It's not weird! That's how it should be! Babies need to sleep a ton in order to grow and understand the world around them. You did the same thing when you were a baby, you're just a little further down the road at this point. But your development stage isn't over yet. You haven't fully matured to the final stage so you need to continue getting that same great sleep in order to reach your full potential.

Outside of overall development, sleep deprivation can impact a teen's metabolism. Without the right amount of sleep, the metabolism and hormones needed to regulate metabolism can be affected. Once the metabolism and hormones are altered, the domino effect begins. Other things can also be affected like your immune system and even functions of the brain, such as memory and decision-making.

You guys, this is insane!

When I was in high school, I used to stay up long hours in the night doing who knows what. I watched TV, I read books, I wrote in a journal, I listened to music, I made scrapbooks, and chatted on the phone, and I did a million different things but none of them involved sleep.

As an adult with all of this newfound knowledge, I look back on my teen years and realize just how sleep deprived I was. My metabolism (for lack of a better word) sucked. I was unhealthy with poor digestion and sensitive skin. My mood was unpredictable and I lacked confidence because of who I was as a person. Add the fact that I was sleep deprived and I was one big hot mess!

I hope you teens will learn from my silly mistakes because the only difference between you and me is the fact that I didn't know any of this information. You're a giant lucky duck because you have access to this book, these words, and a million other books for that matter, and the internet—the freaking internet! You have something that millions of people around the world didn't have at a young age. You, my friend, have information.

So my hope for you is that you'll use it wisely. Be a teenager. Do you. Do the things that you love to do. But for goodness' sake, have some balance. Make healthy choices. Eat nutritional foods (most of the time at least) and get a good night's sleep. Don't be in the percentage of people that say "I'll sleep when I die" because then you're taking away from your performance hours. You need sleep in order to be the best version of you. And if you don't want to be the best version of yourself, well then, we have more to talk about! And that's OK, because it leads us to the next chapter…

Health Tip #1

Find an activity you enjoy. A lot of teens have told me they don't like working out because they've tried running and it's too hard. Or maybe they tried biking and it hurt their knees. Maybe they tried sports and didn't love being on a team. If you have a history of trying an activity and you didn't love it, then fill in the blank with your experience. And guess what? It's totally fine if you didn't love your experience. So what if that one activity wasn't for you. The key to activity is finding the *right* one for you. I personally love running. Some of you might like walking or biking or swimming or yoga or stretching or skiing or snowboarding or skateboarding or any other activity you can possibly think of. You might need to try a couple to find the one you like and that's OK! Just don't give up along the way. I haven't always liked running, I promise. It's something that grew on me over time. So keep trying different activities, I promise you'll eventually find one that suits your style.

Health Tip #2

Being a teen today might mean having a hundred and one things to do on a daily basis. So many of you have schedules that are packed to the max, booked with different activities ranging from school, social time, family time, volunteering, babysitting, homework, and studying, etc. If you're one of those teens, you might struggle finding time for exercise. If you do, make it a point to park in the back of the parking lot wherever you go. When you go to school every day, park the furthest away from the building. When you go shopping on the weekends, park at the very end of the lot. It's a fun tip that gets you a little extra exercise every single day.

Health Tip #3

Be open-minded to new things. Whether it's a new activity or a new food to taste, being healthy requires variety. If you stick to the same foods and same activities every day, you're not going to get an array of nutrients like you would if you were switching it up. You're probably going to overuse the muscles that you're continuously using. And let's be honest, you're probably going to get super bored with the same foods and the same activities. I know I would. That sounds awful. If you develop the trait of being open-minded, you're going to have more healthy choices to pick from. You're going to be in a healthier environment, and overall, you're going to be the epitome of health!

Health Tip #4

Research new foods and go on a food journey. I want you to spend time researching. What foods are out there right now that you haven't tried before? I'm sure there's a million different things your taste buds are dying to get a bite of. Talk to your parents about new foods and tell them you want to go on a food journey. A food journey is *not* a diet. You're just on a mission to try new things. Eat a little differently. Switch up the same foods you've probably eaten your whole life. Who knows, you might even develop a passion in the kitchen! Cooking can be a really fun hobby. You might just get a knack for it.

Health Tip #5

Schedule your sleep in advance. Now that you know how critical it is to get some sleep, it's time to make it happen. Set your phone, your tablet, all your devices to privacy mode between the hours of 9pm–7am. That's a full 10 hours of optimal sleep time so you're not constantly distracted by notifications popping up on your phone. Those notifications are going to be the death of us. If you don't eliminate the distractions, getting yourself to sleep is going to be all the more difficult at night. But I trust that you're going to do this! So once you do, just make a point to go to bed earlier. Some of you just gagged, rolled your eyes, threw the book across the room, I don't know but I know you hate the sound of going to bed earlier. I get it. As a teen, I did too. But it doesn't have to be a drastic change. If you normally go to bed at 11pm, then tonight make sure you go to bed 15 minutes earlier. All week this week, you're going to consistently go to bed 15 minutes earlier than usual. And then next week, you're going to go to bed fifteen minutes earlier again. And then the third week, another fifteen minutes earlier, and the fourth, another fifteen. In four short weeks, you will consistently be in bed an hour earlier than you are right now and you'll hardly notice the difference. Don't believe me? Start tonight!

Chapter 5
It's OK to Be _____

This title is for all my teens out there still playing Mad Libs in 2022. If you are, you're my hero. I used to love Mad Libs!

But in all seriousness, let's play for a hot second.

I want you to go back to the title and fill in the blank. Whatever it is that you identify yourself as.

It's OK to be _____.

Now think about it. Are you loud? Are you humble? Are you selfish? Are you quiet? Are you flirty? Are you spoiled? Are you thin? Are you overweight? Are you attractive? Are you ugly? Are you shy? Are you kind? Are you sad? Are you smelly? There's over a million different adjectives that I could jot down, but it's not up to me to list them. It's up to you to fill in the blank. What do you think you are?

Seriously, go back up and write the word in the blank spot. Once you do, it's OK to keep going…

OK, great! Now that you know your word, know this: It's OK to be that person. In fact, it's not just OK, it's fantastic!

There's 4,800 adjectives in the English language. I'll bet you there weren't many people that used the same word as you. How cool is that?

I know I'm cheesy, but I think that's super cool!

It shows that there's no one else in the world like you. No one.

Authenticity is a beautiful thing, my friend. And if I know you like I think I do, then you may have written a word down that's questionable. Maybe you put a word like "ugly" or "confused" or "stubborn" even. Those are all words I've heard teens use when talking about themselves. And truth be told, I don't love it. I wish that teens had more self-confidence and that's what I'm on a mission to do. But for now, I don't want to change your word. I'm here to tell you that your feelings are valid and maybe at the end, you might change that word on your own. Let's take a look and see.

Confidence Is a Beautiful Thing

Confidence is a beautiful thing too, kid. It really is. Even Oprah Winfrey said, "It is confidence in our bodies, minds, and spirits that allows us to keep looking for new adventures."

Self-confidence is defined as the feeling of trust in one's abilities, qualities, and judgements.

So after reading the definition, I want you to ask yourself: what is it that you don't trust in yourself? You don't trust your ability to do something? Well, that sounds to me like you're just a little nervous about the outcome. Maybe it's something you've never experienced before. Or maybe you're unsure about the quality of work you can produce. Well then, that sounds to me like you need to give it a shot and see what kind of work you can produce!

Lacking self-confidence tells me that you haven't yet met your lifelong best friend. Because that best friend is you. Yourself. You know that phrase "me, myself, and I"? That phrase is coming into play. And I'm so excited to introduce you to this person, because let me tell you, they're going to be with you for the rest of your life, through all the hard things, the fun things, the silly things, the weird things, the things you're unsure of, and the memories that will last forever. You have a new best friend and that person is *YOU*.

You: *"Hello, self."*
Inner consciousness: *"Nice to meet you. How are you?"*
You: *"Oh, I'm doing well. How are you?"*
Inner consciousness: *"Feeling great!"*

Are you guys acquainted now? That's great news, because there's more. When teens are lacking self-confidence, it's often because they feel like they haven't accomplished anything great in their lives yet. I have a hunch that you have though, so let's take a walk down memory lane.

Time for a Throwback

To self-reflect is to think about your character, your actions, your motives, and the experiences you've had along the way. What did you learn? How did it make you feel?

This type of thing might sound cheesy to you, and I get that too. So if you don't want to talk about it, that's totally

74

fine. We can keep this chat right here, in the book, between you and me.

The important thing is that you actually do it. There are grave benefits to reflection and that's because it actually works. The idea of reflecting on growth is, in fact, taught at a very young age and it can be entirely too easy to lose the task if you haven't intentionally self-reflected in a long time.

With that said, I want to acknowledge and reassure the absolute vitality of self-reflecting. We should reflect on ourselves, our actions, our words, our thoughts, ideas, and creative lenses. We should reflect on our experiences, the people we surround ourselves with, and the hobbies we like to do in our spare time.

Why?

Because the process of self-reflection deepens the relationships with the ones we have. It enhances our experiences and strengthens our entire existence on Earth. Reflecting gives us the chance to accept our mistakes, learn how to move on, and think about what we can change in the future. Through reflection, we find our strengths, our weaknesses, our goals, and so much more.

Reflecting is an interesting process because it requires you to look into your past. I've never been one to look back in the past, because to me, it always felt like I was harping on something I could not change—until I learned the process of self-reflection which didn't happen until after my teen years. As always, I want to bring this concept to you now while you're right smack dab in the middle of your teen years, because if you actually give it a chance, I think it might be worth your while.

It's not only OK to look back but it's necessary to look back, as long as you are looking back to see how far you've come. That is the beauty of self-reflection.

It's amazing to see how things can vastly change in a moment's notice. A best friend who you've known for half your life can quickly fall out of touch. You might have a whole new circle of friends today than you did a year ago. Maybe you have a different girlfriend than you had a few months ago. All of those things are fine! But have you ever thought about these changes and what happened that caused it?

It's amazing to see how we hold onto the same interests and passions for years on end. A group of friends who played soccer together since they were five might still be playing in high school ten years later.

These reflections show us how we've changed throughout different seasons of life. They show us who or what has always remained our constants.

There are two types of reflections that you can embrace: short term and long term.

Short-term reflection involves mirroring events that happened recently in your life. This is a great process to remember specific details. It's also great to make immediate changes for fast results.

For example, when starting this book, I had the extremely ambitious goal of completing it in one month. The idea came to me in a dentist's chair (as I mentioned at the beginning), and I was thrilled to get all my ideas down on paper as soon as possible. I wanted to get helpful tips and strategies into the hands of many teens who I believed could really use this information. One week into the book, I was halfway completed, which was incredible progress. By the end of week two though, I had barely made any more progress from the first half. I needed to sit down and process what was causing a difference in my ability to write between week one and week two. This was a short-term reflection that allowed me to address the problem and circle back to my writing immediately. I'm thrilled to say, I finished this book in one month's time.

Long-term reflection, on the other hand, involves contemplating events that happened over a long period of time. For example, at the same time that I started writing this book, I also reflected on my teen years. I'd always wanted to be a writer. When I was seven years old, or maybe eight—I honestly have no idea how old I was, but regardless, I was young—I wrote a book about my bus driver being a werewolf. I even drew pictures for it too. And I self-published it by taping all the pages together and sticking it in my school's library. I don't remember my school's librarian, but whoever it was, that person was a saint. Because the day that happened, my dreams were set on becoming a writer. I wanted real books published in hardcovers all over that library and I knew someday it would happen.

That reflection, being able to think back on a long-term event, and hone in to the exact time that I'd found my passion enhanced my experience of writing this book. That little girl I once was would be so proud. That cute little chubby girl who was so sad, so confused, so unconfident, but so ambitious, and lacking purpose, would be so freaking proud of who she turned out to be.

That reinforcement is exactly why we reflect.

Know Your Strengths

During this reflection process, I want you to take notes of the things you're good at. Sometimes, when asked, it's really hard to answer. Most teens shrug their shoulders and say "I don't know" or "Nothing much." And look kid, I know that answer is a lot easier than actually putting effort into listing things. But this is important! This is your confidence we're talking about and confidence is a necessity just like your health. Building yourself up is so much a priority that we dedicated an entire chapter to talk about it!

Kristen Coyne, M.Ed., Head of School, former counselor in post-secondary education, and my super cool older sister, spends almost all her days working with teens. She says, "Helping students to recognize and understand their strengths is like watching them uncover a hidden superpower! By maximizing strengths, you are creating a clear path to full potential with truly no limit. Knowing your strengths builds self-awareness and self-esteem. It helps to create a powerful and authentic connection to your true self! These characteristics are uniquely your own and there is no one else that expresses these skills in the same way that you can!"

So, my friend, the time has come. Let's list those strengths! Think of 5–10 things you're good at. Maybe it's reading, writing, thinking, running, biking, swimming, board games, video games, dancing, talking, laughing, babysitting, skateboarding, cooking, baking, drawing, painting, sculpting, driving, surfing, and I feel like I could probably list a zillion more things, but it's your turn. Write them down!

Strengths:

1.
2.
3.
4.
5.
6.
7.
8.
9.
10.

The Power of Positive Affirmations

"What did you just say?" I already hear the questions as I'm writing these words.

"Oh, not these again," some of you would say.

Or "What is that?" And that's exactly where we'll begin.

Positive affirmations are statements that you repeat to yourself every day. They're daily statements that remind you of how freaking cool you are. They remind you that you're the baddest cat around, even on days when you're not feeling it.

Here's my favorite thing about these too. They can even help you to accomplish future goals. If there's something you'd like to accomplish, but you haven't yet, you can still say them every day as a daily reminder that you're going to complete that goal. And when you say them, you're going to say it in the present tense, as if it's already happened.

How cool is that? It's like a mind trick!

Let's say you want to be an Olympic gold medalist. (I know this is a pretty wild goal, but hey, I say shoot for the stars, kid!) If you haven't yet accomplished that goal, you're going to say every day.

I am an Olympic gold medalist.

You want to write it as if it's already happened.

Now it's time to combine these goals with the things you already know that you're great at.

Let's say you're a good singer. If you are a good singer and you wrote that down in the list above, let's update your list. You're not just going to write "I'm a good singer" but you're going to say "I am an exceptional singer" or "I have the #1 song on the billboard music charts" pending on what your goals might be. Do you want to pursue a career in music? Or do you just want to continue developing your skills? That part is up to you! But I don't want you to use words like "good" or "decent." I want you to use words like "exceptional" and "fantastic." Look up some adjectives if you have to! These affirmations are going to be the best reminders you'll ever get!

So go ahead and update your list. Add at least 5–10 goals that you want to pursue. Adjust the goals as if you've already accomplished them. Once your list is complete, you should have a minimum of 10 things on your list that shows how freaking awesome you are! It's not only OK to be you but it's amazing to be you! Read them out loud.

Goals:

1.	
2.	
3.	
4.	
5.	
6.	
7.	
8.	
9.	
10.	

Confidence Tip #1

Set the daily affirmations as reminders in your phone. Set them to pop up intentionally throughout the day. Are there times in the day when you need a little bit of extra positivity? Maybe you're bombarded with classes or don't want to go to a sports practice. Maybe you're out with friends and don't want to head home yet. Be proactive in advance and set these intentional reminders ahead of time. They'll pop up and remind you of who you are and who you want to be.

Confidence Tip #2

Be consistent with your affirmations. Don't write them once and look back at them in a month's time. You want to use these to your advantage every day. Some people like to write them down every day, others like to say them out loud in a mirror every day. I've also seen people use post-it notes to place around their desk space or vanity. Do whatever works for you. But make sure you're seeing, reading, writing, or saying these goals every single day. Consistency is key.

Confidence Tip #3

If programming these affirmations into your phone is too daunting of a task, there are affirmation apps already out there that you can download. The apps will do all the work for you and tailor the positive tips to pop up throughout the day. This is a great way to utilize technology to your advantage, support new apps, and build your confidence daily. Your growth game needs to be consistent so an app might just be the perfect fit for you.

Confidence Tip #4

As most of you probably learned in Science class, humans store energy in our bodies and we burn through that energy daily. Many teens lack confidence because their energy is being used to focus on things like anxiety, stress, fear, or anger. Thus, if you know teens who are more confident, it's likely they appear to be more energized people. That is because their body's energy is focusing on other things like goals, challenges, and fun experiences. In order to be a more confident person, challenge yourself to boost your energy levels. If you need to boost your energy levels, go back and read chapter 4. All those health tips like good nutrition, proper sleep, and adequate sunlight will really help to elevate your energy and in turn, boost your confidence.

Confidence Tip #5

Now that you've addressed who you are and learned to accept it with confidence, you should truly be following your passions. Don't follow other people's passions if it's not authentic to what you love to do. Follow your heart and chase the things that you enjoy doing. In your passions, you'll find your confidence and your greatest successes.

Chapter 6
Daydreaming Is Awesome

Even though we talked about living in the moment and listening to people and all those great things that show how you're present and aware throughout the day, daydreaming is really freaking cool too. I'd be lying to you if I wrote a book for teens and didn't talk about the art of daydreaming.

Maybe you read the short story *The Secret Life of Walter Mitty* in English class or maybe you even saw the movie with Ben Stiller. Both forms of mediums are great examples of what happens when a person gets bored with their life. The story was written by James Thurber who talks of a man who's super bored with his life and has a variety of his own self-imposed limitations. Walter Mitty, the main character, eventually triumphs at the end (at least in the film) once he finds the courage to discover his destiny through a string of pretty wild daydreams. It's one of those feel-good stories that make you happy, so if you haven't seen the movie or read the text, I urge you to do so! Especially because it emphasizes my entire belief that daydreaming is totally acceptable. In the story, Walter Mitty spaces out and daydreams in public, which isn't really the time or place for it. *But*, in reality, when at home, or at the right time, it's totally acceptable.

In fact, it's not just acceptable, it's necessary. We need to spend time being caught up in our own thoughts, envisioning things in our minds, and daydreaming until the sun goes down.

This is especially true for adolescents. Daydreaming is such a pivotal part of your growth because it allows you to reflect on your life, the actions you've taken thus far, and the paths you want to go down. Daydreaming allows you to visualize who you want to be in the future.

During these critical teenage years, you're asked a zillion times, "Where do you want to go to college?" or "What do you want to do when you get older?" And deep down, I know you all want to say, "I have no freaking idea. I'm 15 years old, how am I supposed to know that?" And if you've ever answered with that exact response, then kudos to you. I totally support that. However, what you could also say is, "I'm not sure, but lately I've been envisioning my future to have some elements of _____." You fill in the blank. That would definitely be an appropriate way to answer too and it includes you dreaming about the future.

The question that adults should be asking you teens is: "Have you daydreamed about what your life might look like in one year? Or what about five years?"

Oftentimes, we overestimate where we're going to be in one year, but we underestimate where we're going to be in five.

Many times this is true for seniors in high school because you're so focused on graduation and where you want to go to college and what your life is going to look like one year from now. But you don't realize how fast college flies and a five-year-plan not only includes your graduation but it also includes your entire four-year-school and your college graduation too.

Not that I want to scare you into thinking of the perfect five-year-plan, but what I'm saying is not to miss out on daydreaming. You should spend several hours daydreaming about what your life could look like five years down the road. It will enable you to recognize if you like that vision or if you want to change the path.

Live in the present moment, of course, but make sure to daydream. Spend time in your thoughts. Be creative. And dream your days away. What you visualize is what you will manifest, which is what your future will hold.

Daydream about who you want to be and who you want to spend time with. Daydream about where you want to live and where you want to vacation. Daydream about what kind of jobs you might have. And make sure to have multiple different visions.

Dream about yourself in various jobs and various homes and constantly be in various situations because you don't need to have one set course for your life. You can have many. And you *should* have many.

I can tell you first hand I'm 29 years old and I've never had one set course for my life. I still couldn't answer that question "So what do you want to do when you get older?"

Because I'd have a million different answers. I'm a teacher, a writer, a marathon runner, a mom, a wife, a world-traveler. I spent years working as a store manager in retail and I'm super passionate about nutrition and cooking. I have a zillion different paths and you should too. You don't need to have one set thing for the rest of your life. You should have many because you're going to be interested in a zillion things during different seasons of your life.

Now here's the kicker with this too: don't overwhelm yourself and try to envision yourself doing a million things at the same time. You can do *absolutely everything* you want to do. But you can't do them all in the same season of life. You might want to go to college and play on a sports team. You might want to be a lifeguard in the summer and travel in the winter. Just make sure you don't set out to do everything at once. You'd be setting yourself up for failure.

So overall, kid, I think you get the point. Make sure to daydream. Visualize yourself and your future and incorporate a million scenarios into it. It's totally normal if you don't see yourself doing one thing. It's fun to dream about yourself doing a million things and you should. This is what you need to do in order to see where you fit in the world. Find out who you are going to be and what you are meant to do. You are meant to do so many things, so many more things than you could possibly imagine. But visualization is key. It will help to prepare you for the journey ahead.

You Need a Bucket List

It's hard to live a really cool life when you live with your parents. I know, I remember that. You may or may not drive and you still have to go to school every day too. There's nothing cool about any of those things and I totally get that.

We're all going to have different views on what is and isn't cool, but it's up to you to make the vision a reality. Even if you can't live the coolest of cool lives right now, that doesn't mean you can't dream.

When I was in high school, I was so desperate to graduate and move on to the next stage in life that I created a bucket list and dreamed of all the amazing places I'd love to travel. There were so many things I wanted to do like skydive, scuba dive, swim with sharks, and a dozen other really dangerous things at the time that seemed wildly farfetched.

But guess what? Remember when I said the things you believe will manifest into your reality? I've never heard something truer in my life. By the time I turned 25, I had travelled around the world, backpacked through over 35 countries, jumped out of two airplanes, scuba-dived in the Red Sea, and swam with great white sharks off the coast of South Africa.

I sound really freaking cool just typing out those words. But the thing is, I'm not all that cool. I'm actually pretty nerdy and you can tell because I'm the author of this book. I definitely wasn't cool in high school and if you told 15-year-old me that I would accomplish all those things in the next ten years, I probably would've laughed in your face.

Creating a bucket list really helps you to set high expectations for the wild things you'd like to do at some point in your life. Something exciting, something so far-fetched that you're unsure if you'll ever accomplish it. But I promise, it's really fun to do. And a few years down the road, when you do accomplish these things, it'll make your reflection so much better.

I want you to pause in the book right now. Write down all the things you'd like to accomplish at some point in your life. It could be wild and dangerous like mine. Or they could be goal-oriented, family-oriented, whatever is fitting to you.

Maybe you want to have a family and kids? Maybe you want to have seventeen cats? Maybe you want to open up a zoo and run with the elephants? Maybe you want to work for NASA and build a rocket ship? I don't know what your thing is but it's time for you to write it down. I want you to come up with ten great things that sound really exciting to you. If you don't know what they are, then do some research. Look and see what's out there for you to do. The world's a really cool place when you get the chance to explore it.

Bucket List:

1.
2.
3.
4.
5.
6.
7.
8.
9.
10.

We All Need a Little More Hope in Our Lives

Have you ever wanted to go out with your friends and your parents told you "maybe" or "I'll think about it"? If you have, then you know the hours leading up to their answer was full of anticipation and angst because all you wanted them to do was say that one word: yes. You were living in an optimistic state of mind. You were praying, hoping, waiting to get the answer you were longing for.

The feeling of hopefulness is one of my favorite emotions. It means you know what you want. You're not sitting on a fence confused about where you should go. You've made the decision and you're ready to make something happen. To be hopeful is to be full of positivity and to look at the cup half-full.

When you spend time visualizing, it becomes so surreal and you're hopeful that your dreams will come true. Or, you might realize it's not what you're hoping for and you might need to visualize another path. Regardless of how it pans out, the feeling of hope is a powerful tool that will help you to decide what you really want in life and it'll urge you to figure out how to get it.

Accepting this emotion into your life will be groundbreaking because it will make your hard days that much easier to get through. Think about the recent pandemic you just lived through. It was really hard not to see your friends all the time, wasn't it? Some of you lost out on opportunities that you had been excited about. Some of you may have missed sports seasons, or graduations, or other monumental events that you'd been longing for. It feels like you've been robbed of something great.

In order to get through that hard season of your life, I'm sure many of you were hopeful that the pandemic would eventually come to an end. And not only will the pandemic end but there will be many more exciting events in the future. You have to be optimistic and full of hope in order to look into the future and see a positive image. Hopefulness gives you strength. Strength gives you the power to move forward. Be more hopeful and your vision will be clearer.

A Chinese Bamboo Tree Takes Five Years to Grow

There's an amazing story that's been told by a number of people and I'd like to pass it on to you teens.

A Chinese bamboo takes five years to grow. After being planted, the seeds must be watered every single day. It must be watered and fertilized every day for five years. That number is equivalent to 1,825 days. And during those many days, someone must water and fertilize the seeds.

The seeds give absolutely no sign of life, no guarantee that they will sprout into a mighty bamboo sooner or later. And yet, after five years, the seeds break through the ground and emerge as a bamboo plant. And still, it not only breaks the ground but it grows ninety feet in just five short weeks!

So the question arises: does the bamboo plant grow in five years or five weeks?

Well, that answer is simple. It grows in five years.

When you are a teen, sometimes it's hard to visualize the mighty bamboo plant that will emerge in five years. It's easier to focus on what will happen in the next five weeks, rather than five years. But if you have patience and trust the people who are a little older, a little further down the road than you, then I promise you're going to like what you see in five years' time.

Do you think that seed wanted to wait five years in order to grow? Probably not. Do you think that farmer wanted to spend five years watering and fertilizing a plant he couldn't even see? Probably not.

Right now, you're the seed in the ground. Have patience, young grasshopper. Trust the process. When you visualize your future, be realistic. Don't expect things to happen overnight. Know that you will grow into a strong, powerful bamboo tree, but it might take five years in order for it to happen.

Daydreaming Tip #1

Don't give yourself a time limit. When getting started on your visualization journey, you never want to give yourself a time limit. Just get creative and let yourself dream. If you start giving yourself time limits, it might feel overwhelming. The long list of amazing dreams could intimidate you if you tell yourself you only have five years to complete it. So, the moral of the story is to give yourself as much time as you need. Give yourself all the time and refrain from any possible boundaries.

Daydreaming Tip #2

Try to envision yourself as the farmer in the Chinese bamboo story. Do you think you'd have enough patience and consistency to water the same seeds every day for five years? If the answer is no, you might need to practice your resiliency. And if you do, that's OK. Most teens do agree that they would give up after a few weeks because it's not very rewarding to water a plant that you can't see. This is where visualization comes into play. Stop watering something you can't see and instead, see the bamboo plant. Envision it in your mind. Next time you think something is taking too long, imagine a ninety-foot bamboo plant standing in front of you. Do you have any idea how freaking big that thing is? Ninety feet is really stinkin' tall! If you have a massive bamboo plant following you around wherever you go, it'll be a constant reminder that great things take time.

Daydreaming Tip #3

If visualizing is hard to do in your brain, sit down and draw a picture. Many of you teens are super creative and unbelievably talented. Even if you don't agree, I know you have the power to pick up a pencil and draw. Try to envision your future in a picture. What do you look like? What does your house look like? Or an apartment? Or any space you want to live in? Where will you be? Who will be there with you? Physically drawing out the picture will best help some of you artistic and visual teens.

Daydreaming Tip #4

Talk to other people about your future. I'm sure your parents will be thrilled to have a discussion with you because parents love helping out with future goals. If not your parents, talk to your siblings, friends, or teachers. I'm sure there's a counselor at your school who focuses on secondary education, future goals, gap year programs, and any other possible opportunities out there. The more people you talk to, the more information you absorb. The more information you absorb, the greater your vision will be.

Kristen Coyne, M.Ed., adds "If it inspires you and motivates you, chase it! Vision boards are a fantastic and fun tool to support you in transforming your dream to a reality. As my students explore their futures, we always start with a few art supplies, magazines, and a poster board. Together, we brainstorm what it could and might look like for them. It is so important to identify a mentor that can ask the right questions and challenge you to think bigger. Our thoughts and dreams create a world! Create a world that not only inspires you but is truly worth creating!"

The people around you want to hear your amazing, life-sized dreams. Share it with them.

Daydreaming Tip #5

Learn about other people's stories. I'm sure there's someone that you admire, someone whose shoes you'd love to walk in for a day. That person likely inspires you because they're further down the road than you are and you're watching them after their dreams have come true. It's amazing to see other peoples' success, but it isn't fair for you to think they were made a success overnight. Just like you, they probably had to daydream about their success long before they found it. Let's say you admire a well-known actress or a famous musician. Well, they'd probably been dreaming of their success for many, many years before it ever happened. Learn their story. Discover their background and see where they came from. It will help you to see just how big you should dream.

Chapter 7
Everything in Moderation
Is Key

Some of you just read the title of this chapter and rolled your eyes thinking *I will* not *limit my videogames* or *I will* not *spend less time with my friends*. And hey, kid, I totally get it. Sometimes we like doing things excessively when it makes us happy and it makes us feel good.

If you're anything like me, you might even drink coffee excessively because I first discovered it in high school and I was like a toddler tasting ice cream for the first time. *It was freaking amazing.* And of course, I couldn't just simply have a cup a day. I would drink a massive 24 oz cup in the morning and sometimes a second one in the afternoon.

Needless to say, I was not in a state of moderation. And while it was great for the moment, I never realized what excessive amounts of coffee could do to my health.

So, with that said, welcome to chapter 7. I hope you guys are enjoying the book so far, and if you are, that's great! Because it's about to get even better. So far, we've talked about your feelings and emotions. We've talked about the importance of listening, how anxiety is normal, and why you should make your health a priority. We've also talked about visualization, bucket lists, and positive affirmations. These are all extremely important topics vital to being the best possible version of you throughout your teen years.

For this chapter, we're going to dive into a new subject that I think you might enjoy, and that is to have some stinkin' fun! Being a teen is so much fun! At least, it can be if you let it. That's what it's all about. When you're in your teens, you get to do all your *firsts* in life. And that's an amazing thing! You get to do everything for the first time!

You'll probably have your first serious relationship. Hopefully after chapter 4, you'll be trying new foods for the first time and new activities too. You'll be traveling and going on trips and visiting new places, all for the first time. Maybe you'll speak a new language, meet new people, make new friendships, and simply just try *so* many new things. Some of you may even taste alcohol for the first time (not that you should, of course!) but hey, I remember high school. It wasn't all that long ago I was in your shoes. I remember it well. And trying new things was exciting, thrilling, and also scary at the same time.

But here's the thing. I'm not your parent, guardian, older sibling, or anyone who influences your decisions for that matter. I'm just your new friend, Nicole, who's here to give you some guidance through your teen years. So, I'm giving you this disclaimer so you know ahead of time that you do *not* have to take this advice if you don't want to, but I think you should do everything you possibly can.

Yes, you read that correctly and I meant what I said. *Say yes to everything!* But only the first time. (Unless you want to say no, of course.) Remember, if it doesn't raise your energy, your vibration, your spirit, or your bank account, then the answer is no!

With that said, if you come across an activity that isn't an automatic no, then your answer should be yes. Everything is worth a try the first time around. Follow your heart and try everything. The more experiences you have, the better your life is going to be.

Imagine living a life where we didn't experience anything new. That sounds awfully boring if you ask me, so I hope you'll give it a chance.

If you do, then you'll realize there are some activities you enjoy and some you never want to do again. There might be some foods you love and some you want to spit right in the garbage. Regardless of the outcome, you'll never know until you try it.

And when you *do* find things you enjoy, things that you like, things that make you happy, acknowledge it! Congratulate yourself! Maybe go home and jot down in your journal the details of the experience and how it made you feel. But always remember this: everything in moderation is key.

You: But Nicole, what do you mean?

Well, let me give you some examples:

Do you love hanging out with your friends on the weekends? That's great! Continue spending time with them on the weekends. But that doesn't mean you should see them 24/7, all day every day, 365 days of the year. You need time to yourself, time at home, time to rest, time with your family, time to study, and all the other things that you need to do to be a fully functioning human being. This is something that many juniors and seniors forget to do. It's usually the case once a teen gets their license. And I totally get that. Having the ability to drive is fun and exciting, but it doesn't mean you shouldn't go home and rest.

Here's another example. Let's say in the beginning years of your life, you lived under a rock and never had a taco before. Well, you just ate at a new Mexican restaurant and have a new love affair with tacos! First of all, bless you, kid. Tacos are the best darn food on the planet if you ask me! And second thing, it's great that you found a new food to love, but again, it can't be the only food you ever eat. Remember, moderation is key. I've seen way too many teens stick to a very small handful of foods (bread, or crackers, or pizza) and while I totally understand because all those foods sound yummy, you're not getting a variety of nutrients and your body is likely going to be off balance. So when you find new foods that you love (like tacos!), make sure to eat them in moderation.

Here's one last example. Virtual schooling is now a super popular form of education. (Thanks, COVID!) For some of you, going to school on the computer may have been a tough experience. But for others, you may have loved it. And I get that too. You don't have to wake up hours before school. You don't have to shower, get dressed, take the bus, and then get to school and socialize with other people. With online classes, there isn't as much pressure. You wake up and you can stay in your pajamas because no one would ever know. You don't have to go to school and socialize with anyone. You quite literally never have to leave your house. In some ways, it's easier.

I get it.

I understand why some of you love it because some days, I don't want to leave my house either. However, I still make it a priority to get out of the house and spend time outside, connect with friends, family, and do things outside of my four walls. Why? Because moderation is key. If you're someone who loves virtual education, then that is great! But make sure you don't spend all day, every day cooped up inside your house. You need to get outside, see the sunlight, and build relationships with other people.

Now that you have some examples and understand why moderation is important, I hope you guys are as excited as I was when I wrote this chapter. I know, I know, I'm super cheesy so I'm probably more pumped than you are but I think you should be too! You're getting permission to live your life! You're getting permission to say yes to everything and do all the things you want to do! I'm encouraging you to try everything and have a zillion fun new experiences! There's nothing holding you back. You just need to remember that one important thing: moderation is key.

Awareness Is the First Step

In this next section, we're going to talk about boundaries, because in order to have moderation, you need to set limits. However, before you can reach that point, there's one critical step that comes first: awareness. Gretchin Rubin, author of *Happiness Project*, says, "Self-awareness is a key to self-mastery."

The reality is we must all be self-aware as individuals because each of us have unique things that we're passionate about, one of the very things that makes us human.

Remember I told you I drank too much coffee in high school? Well, that wasn't the only thing I did in extreme measures. I also ran *way* too much.

When I first decided to be a runner, it was a difficult decision. I was out of shape, I had asthma, and I didn't have the confidence that I could do it. Still, I liked it. After every run, regardless of how far I got, it made me feel good. It made me feel like I was accomplishing something and working toward a better version of me. Thus, I started running before school, after school, sometimes after sports practice and always on the weekends. I got to a point where I was running at least six miles a day, in addition to playing on a sports team, and I certainly was not fueling myself with the proper nutrition.

I'm pretty sure some of you may have choked or envisioned me with eight heads when you saw that I ran six miles per day in high school. (If I could insert a laughing emoji here, then I totally would!) I know that sounds horrible to some of you but then again, some of you may love to run too.

For me, I had to limit running. Of course, I still ran multiple times per week, but once I became aware of the damage I was causing, I was then able to set a limit. I thought my knees were going to fall off by the time I turned 18.

It might not come quick and easy for you. It didn't for me either. But I'm sure there's something right now that you're doing way too much of. And if nothing comes to mind right away, be open to the idea that it might pop up later. You might be in the middle of doing something, saying something, eating something, and realize that it's an extreme for you.

Let's look at an example. Many teens love cursing.

If you want to curse, then dammit you curse! Research actually shows that cursing can be a sign of intelligence. Oftentimes, we swear as a result of frustration or a physically painful event. When we swear, we are releasing the stress building up in our brain, which helps us to better manage the pain. Now you're armed with knowledge the next time your mom says, "Benjamin, don't curse!" You can say, "It's OK, Mom! Cursing is a sign of intelligence! I'm releasing my stress!" I bet she probably won't have much to say back.

But, all jokes aside, cursing is only acceptable when used in moderation. Cursing is not acceptable when used excessively and you're just spitting out foul language to sound cool. You need to be self-aware of how much you swear, the times you swear, and when it's appropriate to *actually* swear. Only use foul language when feeling certain emotions. Don't throw nasty words around like candy. (Plus, it won't be as fun to swear if you're saying it all the time!)

You might have to do a little soul searching to figure out what your extremes are and that's OK. Put the book down and take some time. Think about what areas in your life might need to set some boundaries, which brings us to our next subject.

Set Boundaries

When you find something you love, it's going to be really hard to limit it. Don't be like teenage Nicole who ran in extreme measures. "But it's healthy" I would say to anyone who commented. I was stubborn and naive, and honestly, I was just uneducated on the idea of balance. It wasn't moderation and I'm still dealing with the stress on my knees ten years later.

Having balance means having mental and emotional steadiness and stability in all four areas of your wellbeing.

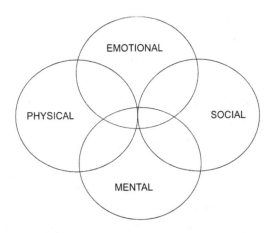

When off balance, things aren't always as smooth as they look in the chart above. Sometimes, we have the mental capacity to process and understand information, but we lack the ability to manage and express our emotions in a relaxed and mindful manner. Sometimes, we have great social experiences, but it takes away from our physical health and the time needed for activity, sleep, healthy nutrition, etc. Or, if you're like me, sometimes you have the power for great physical activity, but it goes too far and takes away from your mental health. You might not be able to process the fact that your activity is too strenuous.

The key to moderation is keeping a balance between these four elements in your life. Become aware of your likes, your dislikes, your behaviors, and which aspects of the chart tend to get out of balance. If you have awareness, then you're already way ahead of the game. Self-awareness is a wonderful tool and it's something I lacked through my teen years. I hope you'll learn from my mistakes and develop this skill early on!

Once you're aware of the things that normally throw off your equilibrium state, name your limits. Create a plan for yourself so you won't fall into the same trap over and over again. Talk about it to a parent, or a sibling, or a friend. Tell them your limits so they can help you out. Never forget the importance of accountability.

The reality is that whenever we enjoy something, we don't want to stop doing it, even if it's hurting us in the end (staying up late and watching TV or playing video games until crazy hours of the night). Don't play, I know you do those things. It's OK, adults like them too. And because we enjoy them, when we finally decide we're going to cut back on them and go to bed earlier, we don't often tell someone else our plans. That way, when you're in the moment and you want to stay up past that curfew you originally set, you don't have someone else telling you to stop.

So remember, awareness comes first.

Boundaries come second.

Tell people in your life what boundaries you are setting so they can hold you accountable. Having an accountability partner will be immensely helpful in sticking to your limits. That way, tomorrow night when you want to keep binge watching *Riverdale* until the sun comes up, Mom can pop her head in to remind you that Netflix will still be there the next day. Besides, when you binge watch a show too fast, it's that much harder to get over it at the end. So spread it out evenly. Limit yourself, set the boundaries, and find an accountability partner.

Addictions Come in All Forms

Recently, I was listening to a podcast that explained addiction and how it comes in many different forms. Most often, we hear the word "addiction" and think of alcoholics or drug-related addictions. This podcast with comedian Whitney Cummings, however, revealed that people become addicted to things like chaos, drama, love, or even heartache.

I found it so fascinating because it's completely true! Your teen years are filled with drama, chaos, heartache, and exciting, exhilarating new things. Think about the people you see every day. I bet you know someone who's addicted to chaos or drama or heartache. Maybe you know someone who's always thrill seeking and looking for a rush of adrenaline.

The truth is we become addicted to these feelings, regardless if it's a negative or positive feeling. If a teen grows up watching a loved one constantly under stress and chaos, then it's likely that teen will adopt the addiction their loved one has. If a teen grows up watching a loved one always in heartache, struggling to find the right relationship over and over again, it's possible that teen might have the same troubling experiences in relationships. If a teen grows up with an adrenaline junkie in their household, that teen might develop the same compulsive desire for adventure. It's an addiction formed by watching other people's addictions.

It's scary but it's also true. So back to the first section in this chapter, awareness is key. Now that you know it's possible to be addicted to feelings, emotions, chaos, drama, and many other things outside of alcohol and drugs, think about your experiences. Is it possible that you could have an addiction?

If the answer is yes, don't be hard on yourself. You have just completed step one by becoming aware. Now it's time to move on to step two and create your boundaries. I believe in you and I know that you're on your journey toward moderation.

Moderation Tip #1

Routines are the best thing since sliced bread. When you have a good routine set in place, you won't feel inclined to go overboard doing the things you like. For example, like most Americans, I enjoy staying up late and spending quality time with friends and family. I do, however, have a sacred early morning routine that can't be disturbed. I wake up every morning before 6 am. I have my coffee, I write, I exercise, I practice gratitude (which we'll get more to in chapter 15). If I don't wake up early and complete my morning routine, I feel rushed and disheveled. I remember constantly feeling rushed in high school. I woke up late and hurried to school. I was rarely on time and my days were always frantic. I needed to change that habit desperately, so I couldn't afford to stay up late anymore. Waking up early, well-rested, to have a calm, relaxing morning is worth sacrificing late nights and television series. Get yourself into a good routine and stick to it. It might take a few weeks to build a routine but you'll be thankful that you did. Your body's circadian clock will naturally kick in and the routine will become a part of your daily ritual. It won't feel forced once it becomes a habit and you'll constantly be in a healthy, balanced routine.

Moderation Tip #2

Keep a journal for your experiences during your teen years. Or at least while you're experiencing things for the first time. You don't have to keep it forever (unless you want to, of course!) But I mentioned in the chapter to say yes to everything! For some of you, that will be easy and fun. For others, that might be difficult and daunting. Regardless of where you stand, I encourage you to keep a journal during this time of your life. Jot down the details of your experiences and how they made you feel. It will be a great practice of reflection, but it will also help you to decipher whether you enjoyed the experience or not. That will make it easier for you to decide whether you want to have that same experience a second time around.

Moderation Tip #3

Focus on the quality of your experiences. If you truly want to create boundaries for yourself and find a state of moderation, the quality of your experiences will be extremely important. Whatever the thing is that you love, if you embrace it in moderation to the fullest quality, you won't be yearning to get back to that thing so quickly. For example, let's use tacos again because I love them so much. Well, every week on Taco Tuesday, I indulge in the tastiest taco you could possibly imagine. I load it up with all the good stuff so that it's a real quality taco and I'm not desperately trying to eat tacos for three days in a row. The quality of the meal allows me to have patience until the following week and enjoy a variety of other foods until then.

Moderation Tip #4

If you believe you may have an addiction to a feeling (stress, chaos, heartache, any type of unpredictable situation) then it's likely you've adopted this addiction from somewhere or someone. Find the root of the addiction. When did this addiction form? Why? Where? How? If there's a person in your life who seems to have similar tendencies, be aware of this connection. If possible, limit your time with that person. Having an addiction to chaos and drama is a real thing, so treat it like that. Limit your time around the people who tend to draw chaos to you and know when enough drama is enough.

Chapter 8
Identity Is a Really Weird Thing

Halloween has always been one of my favorite holidays. Mostly because I think it's funny. What an interesting thing we do every year: dress up as someone else and walk around neighborhoods asking people for candy. If you love Halloween, which I hope you do, then I hope that made you laugh. It's a pretty silly thing to think about. But of course, it's so much fun!

It's the one day every year that we can take on a completely different identity with no questions asked. It encourages self-expression, creativity, and independence. You quite literally have the chance to walk around in someone else's shoes for an entire day.

You take on another identity.

Now, doesn't that sound like an important day to you? The topic of identity is a really weird thing. Oftentimes, teens hate the topic of identity because it's confusing and you don't really know what your identity is. Maybe you have an idea of who you want to be, but you don't think that's who you are yet. Or maybe your parents have a different path that they want you to go down. Or maybe you thought you knew and suddenly, it's changed, and now you might want to go down a different path.

Like I said, identity is a really weird thing. The question of "Who am I?" is such a funny thing to ask ourselves, but the reality is that we all ask it at some point in our lives. It can be a confusing question to answer so I want to prepare you for it in advance.

Halloween does a great job allowing you to try on different hats every year. However, it doesn't necessarily answer the question. So, now I want you to ask yourself: *Who am I?*

If your mind just went blank, that's OK.

In order to begin searching for the answers, you might have to ask yourself a million and a half other questions first. I'll jot down a couple for you to get those brain juices flowing (if that's even a thing).

How is our identity formed? To what extent are we defined by our actions? Or our interests? Or even our talents maybe? Are we defined by the people in our family? Or the circle of friends we have? Are we defined by economic status and social classes? What about religion? Do our spiritual beliefs or our affiliation in a particular ethnic group play a role? What about my region? Does the nation in which we live play a role? How do we label ourselves and how are we labeled by others?

If all of that just blew your mind, then that's probably a good thing. Maybe you've thought of this topic before and maybe you haven't. Honestly, there's no right or wrong answer here. It's all up to you and your perception on the topic. Maybe you like having a specific identity or being tied to a certain ethnic group. Maybe you don't want any affiliations and you don't really know how to define yourself at all.

Regardless of where you stand, no matter what, it's totally OK. But that question of "Who am I?" is especially critical for you teens because you're at a stage in your life where other people expect you to have an answer. And I want to tell you that you don't have to know. But I do think it's important to start thinking about it. Heck, you might choose to never define yourself in one particular way and that's totally fine too. Just do me a favor and start thinking about it. The more you think about who you are now or who you want to be in the future, the closer you'll get to being the best version of yourself today. And once you do have a definition, then I bet a million bucks your confidence is going to grow two sizes too big. (Just like the Grinch did!)

And remember, that's always our goal here: to be the best possible version of you during your teen years. Always know that you're doing an amazing job at this tough thing called life and know that whoever you are, you're a wonderful soul. You have meaning on this Earth, kid, and you're loved dearly.

Facial Expressions, Body Language, and Nonverbal Communication

When talking about identity, it's important to talk about the perception of others. I love asking people "Do you think you're self-aware?" because they always respond with answers like "Absolutely" or "It's one of my best qualities!"

It always makes me giggle because the truth is, we all think we're self-aware. If we answered "no" to the question, then it would basically be a contradicting response. That would mean you're self-aware about not being self-aware. Confusing, isn't it?

If you're a self-aware person, it means you have the power to understand how other people perceive you. And no, I don't want you to drive yourself crazy wondering if people liked your shoes today in school. I'm talking about your behaviors, your emotions, the way you talk, and the things you do. What do your behaviors look like from someone else's eyes?

When you sit down in a chair, do you slouch over or do you sit up straight? When you walk through the hallways, does your body gravitate downward or do you walk tall with your head high? Do you often have your hood pulled over your head or do you look at people clearly? Do you maintain good eye contact in conversation? Do you speak clearly with confidence or is your language usually muffled? Are you often smiling? Are you even aware of your facial expressions to begin with?

Your body language has a grave impact on how others perceive you. Oddly enough, your body language says a lot about who you are without ever having said a word. Don't believe me? Next time you go to school, I dare you to observe your peers. Look at them in the hallways and in the classroom. It's likely you'll be able to tell what kind of day they're having.

Someone who woke up late and rushed to school might appear to be disheveled and walking abruptly down the hall. Someone else might be having the best day ever. They just got a perfect score on a test and are skipping past you to tell their friends. In class, you might notice someone confused by the word problem on the board. You can usually tell by the blank stares and puzzled looks they'll be giving the teacher. Another person might be slouched back in the chair with their hood up, scrolling through their phone. I would assume that person might not be so interested in the class material and they might need a partner to work with.

The things you do are written all over your face like black ink. People notice it because that's what we do. We're humans and we observe our surroundings. The ink isn't permanent though, so if this is the first time you've ever thought about this, don't worry. Moving forward, you'll have a better sense of self-awareness and you'll know to match the appropriate body language with the right situation.

Think about this: I bet sometimes you're so deep in thought, or so engrossed in someone else's story, that you forget what your facial expression looks like. Just think of your favorite movie. You might get so lost in the movie that you don't realize your mouth fell open ten minutes ago.

This happens all the time.

And it's normal. But it can also communicate the wrong message.

If someone is telling you a funny story, then you want to be smiling. Show happy emotions. If someone is telling you something sad, then you want to have a more serious look. Nod as they are speaking. Show that you empathize with them.

This might sound really simplistic, I know, but the truth is that we don't think about our facial expressions or our body language at the moment. Just like most of our previous topics, that means awareness is key. And now that you're aware of it, continue to build your awareness by paying attention as it happens.

Always keep good body posture. Someone who stands tall with their head raised looking forward shows confidence and conveys positive energy. On the other hand, the act of slouching or looking down signals negative emotions.

If you're reading this thinking there's no way you can control your body language or facial expressions when they happen, then think again, my friend.

It's crazy to think these factors could influence our identity. But the truth is that they do. Our identities are influenced by how we *think* others see us. Sometimes, the way people see us and the way we *think* they see us are two totally different things. Being able to measure how people view you is a powerful tool (one that you can definitely add to your toolbox!) and one that will likely help with anxiety as well. Sometimes, we think too tediously about someone else's thoughts, and it can stir up a lot of butterflies in the tummy. To be frank, it could drive you crazy because unless you talk to that person, you'll never know how they really perceive you. Harping on other people's opinions can be a black hole that you certainly don't want to go down, so I urge you to practice this skill.

Now that you have the power of self-awareness, in time, with practice and observations, you'll be able to master the art of body language, facial expressions, and all types of nonverbal communications.

Multiple Personalities Are OK

If you've ever done a biography assignment on a famous person in history, then you could probably do a good job forming their identity. What are some of the things they did? How did they behave? What are they known for?

I remember doing a biography of Princess Diana (some of you might not even know who she is). If you don't, put the book down. We're done here.

(Insert laughing emojis again!)

No, I'm just playing. But in all seriousness, I do remember writing a biography on her and I remember thinking how elegant she was, so humbled, so reserved, so beautiful. It was a part of her identity. It was who she was. A warm, sweet, graceful person.

And then I remember thinking, *Oh, wait. You don't even really know her. And you never will. So why do you have all these wonderful opinions of her?* Well, it was through research and stories that I read about her. But what if that's just the way she appeared in the public eye? What if she was a totally different person in the walls of her own home?

As for Princess Diana, I'm sure in the walls of her home, she was equally sweet, loving, and wonderful. But for many of us, this is a real thing that we deal with every single day. We're on a journey trying to figure out our identities, yet we act differently pending on our changing environment and the people we surround ourselves with.

Have you ever been around a group of friends and acted in a particular way? And then the next day, you're hanging out with another group of friends and you act completely different than you did the day before? I'm sure you have. And don't worry, it's totally normal.

Different people trigger different behaviors. Have you ever heard of that phrase "You are the five people you surround yourself with the most"?

Well, it's a real thing. When you surround yourself with certain people, it's likely you'll adapt the tendencies and behaviors they have as well. But your environment plays a huge role too, so as your environment changes, you'll pick up new behaviors and different tendencies. We tailor our responses to situations and the people surrounding us.

With that being said, be very careful about who you spend most of your time with. Have diverse groups of friends and divide up your time with each of them. We'll get more into this in chapter 12, but the more people you surround yourself with, the more experiences you have. You might take on multiple different personalities, but that's totally fine. Afterall, you're still figuring out this whole identity thing.

Be authentic and stay true to who you are. Diverse relationships allow you to connect with the people that really get you. Diversity allows you to feel less pressure because you're connecting with different people more often.

Understanding History

When we read poems, short stories, novels, and autobiographies, we're learning about the author's identity. Without them spelling it out for us, we can pick up the author's emotions through the tone of the writing. We can pull out pieces that help us to understand history and create a connection between history and the author's identity.

Our identities are affected by our values, our ideas, and our actions. So when writing them down, it helps us to build a better understanding of the world in many years to come.

When I was in school, I always liked to read background information about the author to draw historical context between the piece of writing and what was going on in that time period. It helped me to better understand the author's identity.

I loved doing this for two reasons. One, it made the story relevant on a historical timeline. And two, we got to see the many layers of that author. Most authors have so many other things going on in their lives that inspire them to write. Our identities have a lot of depth to them. In order to understand our own identities and our own depth, writing it down is an amazing way to keep track of who you are. It'll help you to reflect on the past and better understand yourself. Why are you the way you are? Why do you do things the way that you do? Reflecting on your previous identities will help shape the person you are today.

If we're not careful to reflect on the past and intentionally try to form our identity, then sometimes, we let the bad things that have happened to us *become* our identity. We wear those bad things around like a heavy weight on our shoulder instead of leaving it in the past. It doesn't matter how old you are, teens and adults alike can always turn it around once you intentionally begin to shape your identity. You, kid, are ahead of the game by learning this now.

Melissa Cartlidge, MSW and my amazing sister-in-law, has been working with teens and children for over 10 years. She says, "Your identity is not synonymous with who you are (student, child, girl, boy, friend, waiter, etc.). Instead, your identity is built through your actions, which are directly linked to your personal values. Take time to really consider what is important to you (family, love, connection, adventure, courage, health, and the list goes on and on), and allow these principles to help guide you through life."

So, I encourage you to spend a few minutes writing down who you were in the past. This will be especially helpful to you if you're struggling to figure out your identity today. Do a bit more of self-reflection but not just focusing on an experience, focus on *you*.

What you discover will help to better understand your history, your whole self, and who you want to be. There's a blank space below and I want you to use it to explore your identity. Take a few minutes and write down who you think you are. Maybe write down who you used to be or who you want to be in the future. Write down some core values and fun things that interest you. Draw a picture of yourself if you don't have the right words to say. This space is your creative space, so feel free to use it however you'd like. Just focus on understanding your true identity and remember, this is for your eyes only.

Identity:

Identity Tip #1

I know identity can be a scary thing, but be open to the idea of creating it. Many teens shut the idea down because they're too uncomfortable to think about who they are. If you're not who you want to be at the given moment, it's totally fine. You can be intentional about working toward the person you'd like to be. But the first tip is to be open to it. None of the other strategies will help if you don't start by being open to shaping your identity.

Identity Tip #2

Let go of your past. Adding onto the last tip, many teens are uncomfortable with their identity because they associate who they are with negative things from their past. If that's you kid, listen up, because this is important. Your past does not define you. If you've experienced trauma, the trauma does not take the place of your identity. If you're not careful about intentionally trying to form your identity, then you might accidentally let all the bad things that have happened to you become your identity. Don't let negative things control your life. You need to be intentional about reframing your hard days and shifting it into positivity. You have your whole life ahead of you and that's an amazing thing! You can start intentionally molding your identity now. All you have to do is recognize that your past is your past. It's not who you are as a person.

Identity Tip #3

Ask your friends and family for advice. When trying to find self-awareness, you might need some honest feedback first. Ask people around you how they perceive you. When they give you feedback, listen to it. Be open to it. Even if it's not all stars and rainbows, that's OK! We have a lot of time left to practice this skill. Heck, kid, you have the rest of your life, so there's no rush! Hopefully, your friends and family members are honest with you. Then measure their feedback with your own perception. If they see you the way you *think* they see you, then you're off to a great start! You probably do have a good sense of self-awareness. If their perception is totally different from yours, then take their feedback and practice the art of observation and recognition over the next coming weeks.

Identity Tip #4

I mentioned in chapter 1 that there are a zillion personality tests online and there really are. If you want to explore aspects of your identity, one of these personality tests could really come in handy. Understanding why you do some of the things you do could be a really enlightening experience for you. The Enneagram personality test is my favorite of all the personality tests and it's based on nine types of personalities, each driven by their own set of core emotions, fears, and beliefs. After taking various different personality assessments throughout my life, the Enneagram was beyond expectations. It is frighteningly accurate and provides insight to your strengths and weaknesses. I highly encourage you to take this test and identify which type you are. I guarantee it'll be worth your time. It will help you to know your limits and understand your boundaries. But once you can identify with one of the nine types then you're on the right path to understanding your identity.

Identity Tip #5

Take all the time and space you need. Don't rush into an identity just because you feel like you need to. Your identity will forever be changing so know that it's going to take time. Your identity is not formed overnight, it will continue to mold and shift with each new experience you endure. Remember the bamboo that takes five years to break through the ground? Your identity is similar. It might take longer than five years to form, but once you discover it, you're going to love what you find.

Chapter 9
Stop Comparing Yourself

Now that we've talked about your identity and you have a good idea of who you are, it's time to talk about one of my favorite topics. Comparisons!

Yes, as someone who's super passionate about reading and writing, I love talking about metaphors and similes and analyzing different forms of media and all that great stuff that I'm sure is super boring to you, my friend.

Lucky for you, that's not the type of comparison I want to talk about here. Right now, I'm more interested in figuring out how much you compare yourself to other people. Don't play with me either. In today's world, it's all too easy to compare your life to someone else's, to compare your success to someone else's. Thanks to social media, it has never been easier to feel insecure in your own shoes. We spend too much time scrolling through other people's highlight reels that it's easy to lose track of our own highlight reel.

Have you ever heard that phrase "Comparison is the thief of joy"? If you haven't, the phrase is attributed to Theodore Roosevelt, and it's arguably one of the best quotes I've ever heard in my life. I told you his name would pop up again. What a wise human that guy was! His words were relevant in the 1900s, they're still relevant today, and I'm willing to bet they will be relevant 100 years from now.

Why?

The reality is that our society spends way too much time comparing ourselves to others. Whether you compare yourself to a sibling, a friend, a celebrity on TV, a famous blogger on Instagram, it doesn't matter. There always seems to be someone superior, or better looking, or thinner, or more fit, or someone who seems to have it all figured out. Doesn't it seem like that?

Newsflash, it's a highlight reel.

On social media, people don't usually share the bad things going on in their lives. They share the good things, the fun things, the happy moments, and the days where everything's going great. But deep down, you never know what's *really* going on in someone's life behind the string of photos that makes their life look fabulous. The same person who appears to have it all together might actually be struggling. They might be drowning in anxiety or craving connection. Sometimes, people need more support than they let on and I'm sure you know someone who does this. (If it's not you, yourself!)

On the other hand, you don't want to compare yourself and feel superior to anyone else either. Maybe your locker is much cleaner than your friend's locker. Maybe you have a friend who is not the best partner in gym class, but you're really competitive and you like to win. Just like you, the people around you are discovering who they are, exploring their identities, and stepping into their own shoes. Give them grace.

Ultimately, you never want to compare yourself to anyone. It brings on feelings of inferiority or weakness. It can bring on feelings of superiority and judgement. It's unhealthy and it's one of the fastest ways to throw you off balance. (You've worked so hard to balance yourself, so why would you ruin it now?)

Remember the four elements of wellness that we talked about in chapter 7? If not, let's mention them again: physical, mental, emotional, and social. When you spend time comparing yourself to someone else, you're not only impacting your emotional state but you're impacting your social status as well. Why would you want to compare yourself and bring on feelings of inferiority or superiority toward someone you know? That person might be a sibling, a friend, a peer, or anyone else you can think of. Don't you want to maintain a healthy relationship with that person? I would hope you do. And if you answered yes, the best way to do that would be to refrain from comparing yourself to them.

Here's the kicker though: Our society makes it *really* freaking hard to avoid comparisons.

Seriously. It's true. Unfortunately for us, our society does not make it easy to move past this phase. We idolize celebrities in magazines, on TV, all over social media, etc. We see people who seem to have it all together. They have looks, success, money, accomplishments, and probably a million social media followers too. If only we could be like them, am I right?

Wrong!

So wrong!

You guys, we need to stop doing this to ourselves. You need to break this habit now while you're in your teen years because if you don't, this will easily stick with you into adulthood. Comparing yourself to others and negative self-talk is a habit. We need to break this habit and change the narrative immediately. It enhances our anxiety, our depression, our stress. It impacts our sleep, our mental health, the way we see ourselves, and our ability to function. This is everything we've talked about and I'm not going to let it go to waste. So, without further ado, let's get started.

Break up with Social Media

OK, you don't have to break up forever. But sometimes, you definitely need a break. We can all agree that the use of screen time and social media is getting a bit out of control. We have access to the internet at all times of the day and with that, we have access to what everyone's doing all day every day. It's actually pretty wild to think about it.

Instagram stories, Snapchat stories, Facebook stories, and all the stories out there make it possible to capture moments throughout one's day. And then it's held there for 24 hours. We quite literally see what people are doing constantly. It's nonstop.

No longer are the days when you saw your friends at school and didn't see them again until the following day. Now, you leave school and text them, call them, and physically see what they ate for dinner on their Instagram story. No longer are the days when you went through a break up and tried to avoid your ex as much as possible. Now, you go home and watch everything your ex is doing! And we all know your ex is probably making it seem like everything's amazing. They're making it seem like they're totally unaffected by the breakup, which doesn't make you feel good either.

You guys, it's exhausting just thinking about it.

We have constant access to other people's lives, which then results in constant comparisons. Most of the time, it's subconscious and you don't even know it's happening. If you see a friend go off to soccer practice, then you feel guilty for not exercising. You see another friend eating a salad and you feel like maybe you should have eaten a healthier snack.

If it's not your friend's Instagram story that you keep stalking then, it's even worse—it's someone you don't even know. Does anyone feel like that's weird, or is that just me? Why do we compare ourselves to celebrities or models or Instagram bloggers? We literally don't even know them! Why in the world would we compare our lives to one another?

Social media is a very, very small sliver of reality. And yet, it's the picture that is painted in our minds. When we see people's highlight reels, we automatically assume other people have it all figured out. Truth is, they don't. The picture that's painted isn't completely accurate and in many ways, it's likely a skewed image. Nevertheless, research has proven that constant access to social media causes depression, anxiety, poor self-image, isolation, and so many other issues.

In order to break these negative habits, you don't have to purge your social media accounts altogether, but you should take breaks. In fact, it's imperative you take breaks and cut back your screen time.

Practice Celebrating Everyone

I truly believe nothing great ever happens from comfort zones. If you're a teen who tends to compare yourself to others (consciously or subconsciously) then this might be a bit out of your comfort zone. It might even sound really cheesy too, but it's time to start celebrating those around you.

Learning how to celebrate everyone is like a golden ticket out of the comparison world. If you can appreciate good things happening to other people, then you'll never feel any type of negative feelings toward those around you. You'll end up being an overall happier, lighter, more blissful person.

In addition to feeling better, other people will notice your celebrations too. They'll be appreciative and grateful to you for feeling so positively.

You: But Nicole, how do I celebrate someone? What does that even mean?
Me: Don't worry kid, I got ya! Keep reading…

By celebrating someone, you're openly expressing your positive feelings toward them. Acknowledge them for their achievements, even if it's an achievement you didn't yet accomplish. Don't feel negative emotions, just simply be happy for them.

Remember in chapter 2 when we talked about how everyone likes to be heard? Well, this is similar to that. Everyone likes to be acknowledged and everyone wants to be cheered on—even the people who say they don't. So it's imperative for you to acknowledge other people and send all the good vibes their way.

Let's look at a few examples.

Your friend got into the college that you're hoping to get accepted to. You just haven't received your letter yet. Don't worry, your time is coming. For now, celebrate them.

Your teammate scored the goal to win the game. You're happy to win but you thought you were going to be the MVP of the game. Don't worry, you have the next game. For now, celebrate them.

For some odd reason, many of us feel awkward when openly expressing our feelings toward others. Maybe it's because we weren't taught to at a young age. Maybe we didn't grow up surrounded by people who shared their emotions. Regardless of the reason, communication is going to be the most profound skill you will ever use in your life. You need to get out of your comfort zone and learn how to communicate positively toward other people.

When good things happen to those around you, tell them what they need to hear in order to make them feel special. We have one life on this Earth, so why wouldn't we spend every day trying to make people feel their absolute best? Let them know they are royalty. Tell them their worth. Become vulnerable and share your true, raw feelings. For goodness' sake, do not hesitate when kind words come to mind.

Oftentimes, we struggle finding the right words to say, but if you have a moment when the words pop up, do not falter. Do not bite your tongue. Say the words. Whether you're speaking to your parents, a family member, a friend, a mentor, or even a total stranger, it doesn't matter to me! But always go out of your way to make them feel loved.

Tell them they are your hero. You're proud of them. You're grateful, impressed, whatever the words are, just say what you need to say.

People love to be around someone who is present and willing to connect. People like to feel heard and listened to. People love to be acknowledged, so get out of your own way and give them an acknowledgement statement.

Just think about the last time someone made you feel good. What did they say? Did they tell you they were proud of you? Did they tell you they were grateful to have you in their life? Or maybe they complimented your outfit because you were rocking those brand-new shoes you bought last weekend. Whatever it was, that kind soul stepped out of their comfort zone and brought you happiness. Don't you think it's important to provide that same happiness to other people too?

I hope you agree.

Being vulnerable and honest with those around you will be one of the foundational steps in building positive relationships and getting rid of that awful urge to compare yourself to someone else. When you learn how to communicate, connect, and celebrate someone, it really makes everyone feel valued.

Tap Into Your Subconscious

I've mentioned your subconscious a few times in this chapter and I think it's important to acknowledge why your subconscious mind plays such a huge role in comparisons. In order to understand, it's probably best to start from the beginning.

Remember that Austrian neurologist Sigmund Freud we mentioned in chapter 3? Well, he comes up again. Freud was a mastermind and truly advanced the field of psychology. He created many theories of psychoanalysis, including a theory that explains human behavior. Freud created a three-level mind model that divides your mind into three areas: conscious, unconscious, and subconscious.

Your conscious mind includes everything you're aware of. Your thoughts, your actions, the things you see, taste, touch, and feel.

Your unconscious mind includes your past experiences, your memories, and things that pop up automatically. Most of the time, your unconscious is out of reach and you cannot access it. An example of this would be your first words or the first meal you ever ate. You were there, you experienced it, and it's a part of your memory, but no matter how hard you try, you can't remember it. Or when you're in a conversation with someone and you completely forget what you had to say to them. Don't you just hate that? I know I sure do. It drives me crazy!

Your subconscious mind, on the other hand, includes your reactions, the way you behave, your automatic responses, and it's a part of your mind that's completely accessible. As soon as you think about why you did something, you access parts of the subconscious mind. It also makes up roughly 95% of your mind. It's always alert, it's constantly working, and it even speaks to you in your dreams. Its role is to fit a consistent pattern with your behaviors and oddly enough, it learns through habituation.

That last line says it all. If something learns through habits then wouldn't it make sense to have good habits instead of bad ones? If you have bad habits like staying up late, thinking negative thoughts, or comparing yourself to others, then one day, it's going to become habitual. It's going to be a natural occurrence in your brain and your subconscious is going to do those things for you without you being aware of it.

Leon Ho, founder and CEO of Lifehack, says, "Your subconscious mind houses your fears, anxiety, memories, beliefs, and what's real to you. Your subconscious mind is so powerful that it can bypass your awareness to channel the course of your life."

Truth is, you have the power to control your subconscious, but it doesn't happen overnight. In order to trick your brain into positive thoughts, constantly using the tools and strategies in this book will help you to develop a healthy subconscious mind. We're also going to tap into it here.

Below is a box where I want you to pick out one word. One word that you feel like you'd like to know more about. Maybe you have a certain feeling toward that word but you don't know where it came from. Maybe you need to find the root of a biased perception. Or maybe you just want to explore a certain word and learn more about it. It's up to you. Some examples include: food, friendships, family, education, anxiety, support, success, mental health, comparisons, social media, and exercise. Now it's time for you to pick the word. Once you do, you're going to write every single thing you know about that word around it. It might take a few minutes so take your time. You're tapping into your subconscious mind to discover everything there is to know.

Tap Into Your Subconscious:

Once you've completed this activity, it's likely that you pulled out some information that didn't occur to you so quickly before. I hope you were able to find the root of your beliefs in regards to that one word and I hope you have a better understanding of your brain and how it stores information.

If you are someone struggling with comparisons and you feel like you're constantly comparing yourself to someone else, do this exercise again. Dig up the reasons why you feel this way. Find out everything you know about comparisons. Discover why you do this to yourself. Then you can replace those negative thoughts with different habits. Follow the tools in this book and you'll create the healthiest and happiest subconscious mind than any other teen!

Comparison Tip #1

Stop consuming media that doesn't serve you. Stop following anyone on social media who makes you feel bad about yourself. Social media is the devil when it comes to comparisons. Half the time you scroll through your newsfeed, you feel some type of negative emotion because other people's lives look so fun and perfect, and *that Kim chick is so pretty, and why can't I be like her?* Wrong, wrong, wrong! If there are certain accounts that trigger unwanted emotions, pull out your phone right now and stop following them. Hit the unfollow button. Don't play with me either, kid. Do it. You'll be so much happier that you did.

Comparison Tip #2

Prepare your social media breaks ahead of time. Like everything else in life, when you plan for something, the process always seems to go a bit smoother than if you didn't plan for it. Come up with routine breaks that work best for you. Only you can decide the structure of the break, *just make sure you actually take the breaks*. Here's a few examples that you could choose from: Go 3 days on and 1 day off. One week on, one week off. Or you could create an amazing habit for yourself and only allow social media time 1 hour per day. If you tend to be pretty bored around 4 pm after school, let that be your social media hour. Scroll all you want for the hour, but once your time is up, put the phone down and give yourself the rest.

Comparison Tip #3

After planning for your break, set your phone, your tablet, all your devices to privacy mode during the duration of your break. It will be easier to sustain a social media hiatus if you're not constantly distracted by notifications popping up on your phone. I mentioned this in chapter 4, but those notifications are going to be the death of us. If you don't eliminate the distractions, getting a rest from social media is going to be nearly impossible.

Comparison Tip #4

Give out compliments like candy. I can't stress this one enough. People love to feel acknowledged so do it as often as you possibly can. Acknowledge people, celebrate them, and give them compliments as often as possible. If this makes you uncomfortable, it's OK. That means you're growing and it's going to be good for you. Start by giving one person a compliment per day. If you can do that for a week, then focus on two compliments daily. Once you develop the habit, you'll grow from there. They don't have to be large compliments either. Simply tell your mom she made a great dinner or tell your brother that you're proud of him for winning his baseball game. A small compliment goes a really long way.

Comparison Tip #5

Envision your old self as a person. Today is the oldest possible version of you and tomorrow, you'll be even older. That means yesterday you were younger and a year ago you were practically a toddler. (Just kidding, but you get the point!) Your former self is the only person you should compete with. That person you were yesterday didn't know all the knowledge that you gained today. Focus on being a better version of you every single day and you'll stop focusing on other people. Today, strive to be better than who you were yesterday. And tomorrow, strive to be better than who you are today. Continue this practice every day and you'll forget about comparing yourself to anyone else.

Chapter 10
Change Is Inevitable

Ya'll know this already but I'll keep saying it because I'm sure most of you can relate. When I was in high school, I wasn't confident with who I was. Oftentimes, I found myself frustrated with my parents, my sister, my teachers, my friends, or plenty of other people, I'm sure. I always felt like the world was out to get me.

I think more than anything, I was sad and confused and definitely a little angry. People were always telling me what to do and how to feel and I never felt like I was guided in the right direction, which amplified my emotions times a zillion.

One of the most profound things I learned after graduating high school, and I only wish that I had a mentor who could have told me sooner, was that as much as I wanted to, I couldn't change other people. It's simply not a part of life. We can't change anyone else and we shouldn't either. It would be stealing away from their human experience.

With that said, sometimes we have moments when we *do* want to change other people. And if I had a mentor in high school, I would have wanted them to tell me that in order to change my world and the people around me, I had to change myself. There are some things in life that are simply out of reach, but your own mindset is not one of them. We cannot control everything but we can certainly control our thoughts. Thus, in order to change the world around me, I had to change myself.

Had I learned this in high school, I believe my teen years would have been gravely different. I would have been more flexible and more adaptable. I would have been more open to change; however, I often felt like it wasn't my responsibility to change. Most of the time something happened, I thought it was someone else who made a mistake, not me. I thought their mistakes affected me and *they* were the ones who needed to change. I'll say this over and over and over again, but I was wrong, I was wrong, I was wrong.

And if you've been living through your teen years feeling the same way, I hate to be the one to break it to you, but you too, my friend, are wrong. And that's OK, kid! You will learn many times throughout your life that you're wrong. We can't always be right. And truthfully, that's a good thing. It means you're growing and changing and evolving into a more mature, more experienced human being.

Change is a necessary part of growth, and even though most of us hate the idea of change, it can actually be a fun and exciting thing too.

Recently, someone told me "I wish I knew you when you were in high school" and I couldn't help but laugh.

"Oh no, you don't," I said.

And that person said, "Oh yes, we would have been great friends!"

And I replied with, "No, we wouldn't have. Because I was a totally different person!"

It was the truth. I *was* a totally different person. And I'm eternally grateful for opening up to the idea of growth because for someone who used to hate change, I love it now. I welcome change and work hard to learn from it.

For the most part, we don't like it because we're scared of it. To change is to move into the unknown. If we stay the same, it requires less effort and we already know the outcome. But remember I told you nothing great ever comes from comfort zones? If you truly want to be the best version of you during your teen years, you need to start welcoming change with arms wide open. Not sure how to do that? That's OK. We're going to get started.

Emotional Change

When I was in high school, I thought my emotions were a part of me. I was a hot head, someone who acted on impulse, and got too emotional too fast.

"You are who you are," I would tell myself as a way to cope with the fact that I didn't particularly like myself. I especially didn't like the way I acted.

Then I learned that my emotions are *not* who I am. My emotions are simply something I was feeling. They were not my actions. If I could acknowledge the emotions that I was feeling, then I could change my actions. I could change my body language and the other responses that I didn't like.

If this sounds like you, then you're going to like this section. You, my friend, can also change the emotions that you feel. Your feelings do not define you. They're just temporary and you have the ability to control them.

Emotional Intelligence is the capacity to be aware of, control, and express one's emotions, and to handle interpersonal relationships judiciously and empathetically.

Understanding your EQ, which is just like IQ, but all about your emotions, will be critical on your journey of growth. You need to examine your EQ if you want to understand your emotions better and embrace the change that needs to happen.

Sometimes, we are all too lenient with ourselves and don't want to acknowledge that we can use some work, so I want you to envision seeing yourself from someone else's shoes.

What do you look like from your parents' eyes?

What do you look like from your siblings' eyes?

What do you look like from your friends' eyes?

What do you look like from your teachers' eyes?

What do you look like from your coach's eyes?

Do you like what they see?

If you *do* or you *don't*, both are totally fine. Regardless of your answer, we have some work to do, but don't worry. There's plenty of time.

Below, you'll see a link to an Emotional Intelligence test from the Greater Good Science Center at the University of California, Berkeley. In my experience, this test is great for teens because it's based on facial expressions and learning how to read basic signals of the face. You're going to pause in the reading and take the test to see where you stand now and what you can do to better understand your emotions. The more you can understand yourself, the easier it will be to influence those around you and help them to be better too.

As a teen, I'm sure it's really hard to pick a few characteristics that describe you. After talking about identity, maybe you have a few already lined up and a better idea of who you are as a person. But I truly believe there are three traits that are absolutely vital in making it through your teen years: flexibility, adaptability, and patience.

A teen who is flexible can go with the flow during unexpected occurrences. They can change perspectives easily to be more understanding of others. A teen who is flexible does not feel interrupted by change. They are resilient and have the ability to empathize with others.

A teen who is adaptable is a team player and can adjust to new positions. They are compliant, open-minded, positive thinkers with multifaceted skills.

A teen who is patient has the capacity to prioritize their emotions and their tasks. They tolerate delays in schedule whether expected or unexpected. A teen with patience always remains calm. They are gentle, compassionate, caring people. They choose their words carefully and they speak with grace and eloquence.

These three traits very clearly go hand-in-hand. There is no surprise that they are synonyms for one another and they're all great characteristics to jot down on a job application or your future resume.

Now that you've taken the EQ test and you know where you stand, you have more knowledge on your emotions. Keep in mind that your emotions will change as you continue to change. If you want to have a better grasp of your emotional health, practice those three traits daily. Write them down if you have to. You are flexible. You are adaptable. You are patient.

You Should Be Laughing at Your Younger Self

Change is overwhelming and it should be. Nobody likes change. I know this for a fact because just about everyone I've ever met hates change—both teens and adults alike. Even when I reflect back on my own teen years, I, too, hated change. It's simple, most of us hate change! And that's normal because change is the evolving process of something that you have not experienced before. Change can be scary, frightening, intimidating, and it should certainly be overwhelming.

I truly believe in order to benefit in life that you need to go through new experiences that will enable you to change. If you don't go through seasons that challenge you, how will you ever even know the scope of what change really is?

Remember in chapter 7 when we talked about experiencing as many new things as possible during your teen years? Well, we're going to do a full circle here and talk about that some more. But we're not just going to talk about the fact that you *should* say yes to everything, we're going to talk about how you should go through these experiences with the willingness to learn.

Every day that you wake up, you experience a whole new day on Earth that you've never experienced before. That means every single day you are changing. It's inevitable because change is constant. And yet, many teens don't feel like they've changed because they might not have something new to experience every single day.

With that said, imagine if every day for the next month you woke up and ran a mile. The first few days might be really tough, but by the end of the month, you've probably turned into a running professional because you've done it so many times by then. You'd probably look back on your first day and laugh at how naive you were. Because by your 30th day, you've become an experienced runner.

That's how experiences work. Just think about school and a subject you've learned. Take multiplication for example. When you were in third grade and you saw a multiplication table for the first time, it probably looked like a foreign language to you with symbols and lots of crazy mumbo jumbo on it. By the time you hit high school, you could multiply any number off the top of your head without ever having to look at that crazy foreign table again. We laugh at our former self when we've grown enough and we know that we've changed into a more experienced person.

So, again, my challenge to you is to have as many experiences as possible. But don't just do them to do them. Go through the experiences with a willingness to learn so that you can come out on the other side smarter, stronger, wiser. You'll be a more experienced, more mature version of you who's ready to laugh at their former self.

When I was young, and I mean real young, I didn't understand the concept of time. I would ask my parents "Is today tomorrow? Is tomorrow today? What is yesterday? Is that tomorrow?" Haha! Every time I think about it, I totally laugh at myself. The concept of time has always blown my mind, but it's funny to think that I didn't understand how the days change over time.

Do yourself a favor and think of something you didn't know before, and now you do. Go ahead and giggle at yourself. Laughter is medicine. Sometimes, we all need to laugh at ourselves for the silly things we did in our past.

What Do You Value?

We're all taught certain values in life. Maybe you were taught to say please and thank you. Maybe you were taught the golden rule, to treat everyone the way you want to be treated. I was taught the art of creativity and the importance of responsibility. There's dozens of examples I could list here for you, but instead, I just want you to think of some of the values you were taught when growing up.

Your core values are your fundamental beliefs and it's likely you live your life according to those beliefs. Thus, if you value the importance of punctuality and reliability, you're probably a person who's always on time for school. If you value honesty and integrity, you're probably someone who doesn't do well lying and you probably don't love it when your friends tell you secrets that you have to hide from others. If you value kindness and compassion, you're probably a very sweet person, friendly to everyone, easy to talk to, and you empathize with others.

Take an inventory of what you value and recognize that your values are going to evolve over time. What you value in middle school might be spending time with your friends and connecting with peers every day. What you value in high school might be playing sports, getting active, and trying new activities. When you get to college, you might value your education and the thought of exploring your identity. Later in life, you might value traveling, your family, and self-care.

There is no right or wrong order here, I'm just showing a flow of how your values will change during different seasons of your life. So right now, I want you to pause in the book and take an inventory of your values. Ask yourself that silly little question "what do you value?" and jot down your values in the space below.

Values:

Change Tip #1

We are forever in a state of change and we are forever in a state of growth. Yet many teens are so scared of change and so scared of growth. Why? Why are we scared of growth? Why do we push it away? Growth should be welcomed with open arms because it means we experience new things and become a better version of ourselves. Stop looking at growth like it's a nerdy or tacky thing. You should be open to growth and happy to receive it.

Change Tip #2

Change will become easier when you get in the habit of documenting it. Name the change as it happens and write it down. Then, name the emotions that you're feeling and write it down next to the change. This allows you to process the changes that you're experiencing and understand how it's impacting you. Awareness is an important factor when embracing change. If you're aware and able to document the change, the process will move much smoother.

Change Tip #3

I'm going to keep saying this until you get sick of me (Just kidding, I hope that doesn't happen!) But you need to put yourself out there more. Apply for contests, awards, races, and challenges. In order to grow as a person and become the best version of yourself, you need to overcome hard obstacles. If you don't, you'll never know how much you're truly capable of.

Change Tip #4

Remember, if you want to change the people around you, you have to change yourself. Talk to someone you trust about what you want to improve on. Maybe you have a mentor or maybe you want to talk to a parent, a sibling, a friend, or a grandparent. Regardless of who it is, talk to someone who can give you some feedback. Tell them what you'd like to improve on and why. They can help you make the changes in your life and hold you accountable to do so.

Change Tip #5

For some odd reason, teens transition into adulthood at the age of eighteen. Even when I was a teen, I've always found that to be a ridiculous statement. Teens are bright, vibrant, and mature at the age of eighteen, don't get me wrong. But recent science suggests that brain development doesn't fully mature until the age of twenty-five. This is a clear sign that you need to give yourself enough time when you want to improve on something. Think about the ginormous bamboo plants if you have to. Never give yourself a time limit. Just give yourself all the time in the world. You will be able to change your world, which will ultimately change everyone around you.

Chapter 11
Stop Believing the Lies

A long, long time ago, you were a baby. It's a pretty funny thing to think about and I'm sure you've never tried to envision yourself in baby form. Sure, maybe you've seen some photos of yourself, but it's likely that you've never tried to picture the sight of baby you crawling around the kitchen floor. It's a good laugh when you really think about it.

You *were* a baby though, and for the first several years of your life, your brain acted like a giant sponge. Maria Montessori, Founder of the Montessori Method of Education, says, "The development that is taking place during a child's first six years is enormously important. Children develop 85% of their core brain structure by the time they are five years old. A child will now build on this core foundation for the rest of his or her life."

With that said, we all went through this experience. We absorbed information rapidly during those first few critical years as a child. Of course, our brain has continued to grow since then, but especially at a young age, we soaked up everything from our surroundings. Our environment, our family, the interactions we witnessed, the foods we ate, the toys we played with, absolutely everything was absorbed into our tiny brain as information.

Somewhere along those lines, maybe even after those critical years, we absorb these unwritten rules known as societal expectations. Based on the perception of others, we're supposed to act a certain way, think a certain way, dress a certain way, and so on. Sometimes, these expectations can be great and work best for everyone. For example, when you go to the movies, we're expected to wait online to purchase a ticket. We're also expected to turn off our phones and keep silent during the film. These behaviors tend to work out for everyone in the theatre.

Yet, there are other examples that don't exactly work in everyone's favor. A teenage girl should have a boyfriend. She should be sweet, nurturing, help her mother to cook dinner, and love the color pink. A teenage boy, on the other hand, should be confident. He should pay for the meals on dinner dates, learn to repair cars, and like the color blue.

The craziest thing about these expectations is that as a result of them, many teens formulate opinions about themselves. They feel like they're doing something wrong because they don't naturally fall into society's one picture-perfect image. The truth is, you're not wrong. It's not your fault that our society has portrayed one picture for all teen boys and one picture for all teen girls. If you're a girl and you don't like the color pink, then do you, girl! (My favorite color is orange!) And if you're a boy who doesn't want to repair cars or get your hands dirty, then who cares! (I wouldn't want to either!)

You, my friend, are more than enough. You need to stop doubting your presence on Earth. Stop doubting your potential in life and stop doubting who you are as a person. You are enough just as you are, right now.

Some of these societal expectations are a bunch of lies that have been floating through your minds for as long as you can remember. Some of you might not even realize these expectations because you're so used to them that you believe in the expectation too. Regardless of where you stand, I'm here to point them out to you. I want you to know that you don't have to believe everything you absorbed at a young age. I want you to turn a new page and formulate your own opinions on these various topics we're about to jump into.

By the end of this chapter, I hope you'll believe me when I say that you are enough just as you are. And I hope you'll learn that blue doesn't represent the color of boys and pink doesn't represent the color of girls. Next time you have a baby cousin or a sibling born into the world, think twice about what colors you give them. We're here to break societal expectations, not enforce them!

You're Limiting Yourself

Those social norms I mentioned above are basically a bunch of crap. I might get some backlash on that but in my opinion, it's true. As a society, we're failing to show you teens the true values that actually matter. Unfortunately, our expectations revolve around the image that we want to generate and our society cares more about looks and fame and who has the most likes on an Instagram post.

We've shown young men that they can't show their emotions because it takes away from their masculinity. We've shown young women that they're unequal to men and they don't deserve to get paid the same amount.

If you ask me, it's super freaking ridiculous and I'm here to change that. So this section is for the fellas who think they're too masculine to show your feelings. It's for the girls who think that they have to look sexy when they work out. It's for the teens who think they need to date someone because their family constantly asks if they have a partner. It's for the boys who think they need to provide for a future family and it's for the girls who feel insecure to pursue a career.

You guys are following paths that society has laid out for you and I hate to be honest here, but you're doing it wrong. If you follow these paths simply because you feel obligated, then you're limiting yourself. Forget those societal expectations and instead, follow your heart. Be the person you want to be and pursue your true potential. If your heart happens to follow some of those social norms, then that's awesome! But if it doesn't, then don't be ashamed to be your true, authentic self. Social norms shouldn't keep you from living the life you were meant to live.

You have permission to be who you want to be. Stop limiting yourself and follow your gut. I'm sure if you've been believing in the lies that society has fed you, it's possible you've been ignoring your instincts. It's time that you step into the shoes that you were meant to fill. You need to do it for yourself. You need to do it for everyone around you. You need to do it for the world. If you don't, no one will ever see your full potential. And we want to see it, kid. We really do. We want to see your true, raw potential.

Who Told You That You're Not Good at Something?

A few weeks ago, I went to play a game of ping pong and the first thing I said was, "I'm not very good at this."

My friends encouraged me and said, "Just play a round. Give it a chance!" I was reluctant, but I did it anyway.

Needless to say, I was very surprised with the outcome. Turns out, I'm pretty good at ping pong. (I was actually the undefeated champion of the night!)

But that night, I started thinking about the last time I'd played ping pong. Years had gone by since my last game and through all this time, I believed I was a bad player. When I finally remembered the last game I played, I remembered the friend I was playing against and how they were jokingly trash-talking me. They told me I wasn't a good player in an attempt to get in my head and distract me from the game. It was all in good fun, I'm sure, but I naively believed it to be true.

I let those silly words "You're not good at ping pong" sink into my brain and I subconsciously believed it for years.

When I realized what had happened, I was baffled. How did I let someone's tiny comment stick with me for years? The crazy part was, I had totally forgotten about the original comment and believed it to be true myself. Since then, I've been on a mission to dig deep and discover all the lies I'd been told over the years that I subconsciously believe. And unfortunately, I know I'm not the only one guilty of this, especially considering most of the lies stemmed from my teen years.

So now I want to ask you that same question that I asked myself: What lies are you subconsciously believing that someone once told you?

Maybe somewhere along your journey, someone once told you that you were a bad communicator, or a bad friend, or a bad athlete, or a bad writer, or a bad reader, or a bad sleeper... I don't know. Fill in the blank for you. But I'm willing to bet there's some negative thought that you believe to be true about your life, but you were never even the person who planted that seed. Someone else likely made a comment and you have naively believed it ever since.

I'm here to tell you that it's not true. Whatever that thing is for you, stop believing it. I wish I could insert those handclap emojis in between every word. If I could, I totally would. Stop believing the lies.

These lies simply aren't true. Or maybe they were true for a split moment in time, but you know after reading chapter 10 how fast we're all changing. Just because you might not have been great at something in the past, doesn't mean you aren't great at it today.

In order to break this habit, I want you to write down all of the things you believe you're bad at. Have some fun with it too. A few weeks ago, I would have definitely written ping pong in the box. But this is your box (not mine)! So, go ahead, and jot down everything you *think* you're bad at.

The Lies:

Now that you've listed the few things you believe to be bad at, you have one more task. Next to each word on your list, you're going to write this next to it: This is a lie.

It might sound cliche to you but believe me when I say *the things you write have power.* The words you speak to yourself have power. If you continue to believe in these lies, you will continue to be "bad" at them. You're reinforcing the negative things that other people decided for you and that's not being true to your awesome, authentic, teenage self.

I say challenge the narrative and change your perspective. If you do, you'll recognize that these were lies someone once told you. You'll realize it's not true and that you have ultimate control over your mindset.

You're Allowed to Move on to Something Else

I'm sure you've all been told to "never give up" at some point in your life. This is ultimately meant to be a positive phrase that teaches teens about resilience and following your dreams. While yes, it is imperative to work hard and never quit on your dreams, but that doesn't mean your dreams don't change.

I remember being a teen and I was so excited to play sports in college. I loved field hockey, and lacrosse, and being a part of a team. I loved my teammates and how much fun we had at practice together. I was really excited to play in college and to continue that same feeling on a different level.

But then something happened. When I got to college and started playing, I had lost my dreams to be a collegiate athlete. My dreams shifted from playing sports to traveling. I wanted to go abroad and see the world and I simply couldn't do that at the same time as playing two sports at a collegiate level. I needed to work in order to save up the money and as a two-sport-collegiate athlete, you don't have much time for a job, never mind time to go backpacking through Europe.

By the end of my freshman year, I decided I didn't want to come back for a second year. I was so ashamed and embarrassed because I felt like I had given up on my dreams. I didn't want to tell anyone that I quit and I certainly didn't want to admit defeat to myself either. It wasn't until years later that I realized I was entirely wrong. There was nothing wrong with my decision to move on from my athletic career. I wasn't giving up just because it was hard. No, that would have been very different. Truthfully, I grew out of it. I had a new dream that was bigger and more important during that season of my life. That passion I developed for traveling became the major focus of my life for the next several years after I stopped playing sports. And that passion for travel is how I met my husband, which ultimately created the beautiful family we have today.

What I want you to learn from this is that sometimes your dreams are going to change. I mentioned in chapter 6 that you're going to have a million different paths in your life, which means you're going to have a million different dreams. You can follow all of them if you'd like but you can't do all of them at once. Sometimes, you might realize that you've grown out of one dream and another one is taking precedence in your life. When that happens, don't have a little angel standing on your shoulder saying "Never give up!"

No. Ignore that chick. You're allowed to move on at times that are necessary. Just make sure you think it through thoroughly. Weigh all your options and guarantee that it's the right decision.

When it's time to give up on a dream, it doesn't always have to be a time filled with guilt and shame and embarrassment. Not at all. It just means you've moved on to another dream.

With that said, it's not always time to give up on a dream just because you temporarily lost interest. Most people have a dream and give themselves a time frame in order to accomplish that goal. I think that's absurd. If you really want something to happen, then why would you give yourself a deadline?

Stop giving yourself time frames. When you do, you feel obligated to accomplish your goal in that time period. And if you don't, you tend to give up. How unfair is that? You're not giving yourself enough time to develop those skills.

Let's say you want to learn how to play baseball next year. Then you tell yourself, "If I don't make the team after the first year, I'm never trying again." You guys, that's crazy talk! In order to develop the skills needed to grow into a baseball player, you can't give yourself a few months' time and then a deadline. It might take you a year or two before you develop those skills. But who cares how long it takes? Just focus on learning baseball.

Your confidence works the same way. Let's say you want to be a more confident person. Don't give yourself a finish line and say, "I will practice positive affirmations for a month. If they don't work, then I'll stop." You guys, you're creating your own barriers and giving yourself a time period for when you're allowed to give up. Just focus on building your confidence moving forward. In time, eventually, it will happen.

The phrase "never give up" is optimistic and will hopefully inspire you teens to stay consistent. But in an odd, twisted way, teens have changed this phrase into thinking they can never move onto other dreams. They feel guilt and shame when they want to move onto another dream.

Don't believe the lie that you can't move on when it's your time to do so. You have permission to move on and that doesn't mean you're giving up. It doesn't mean you're a quitter. It means you're growing and you're ready for the next phase of your life.

With that said, stop putting finish lines at the end of your dreams too. Just focus on the dream itself. Keep pushing forward and stop counting down the days until your deadline is up. If you ever come across a time where you want to move on to something bigger and better, think it through thoroughly. Make sure it's the best decision for you and if it is, don't feel shame or guilt when you do. Sometimes, moving onto another dream is the right path and it will lead you to something incredible.

Stop Believing Lies Tip #1

Think about the societal expectations that you've learned and adapted. Are you one of the boys who think they can't show emotions? Or are you one of the girls who feels insecure to pursue a career? Or are you someone who doesn't even feel comfortable being your true self? Being aware of specific societal expectations is the first step to reversing the mindset. Once you're aware of it, you can research the expectation and learn the history of it. Where did it come from? Why does our society behave a certain way? What image are we trying to generate? If you understand the root of the expectation, it will be easier to put it into your own perspective.

Stop Believing Lies Tip #2

We're living in the 21st century, which means even though some of these concepts are new to you, we're not inventing the wheel here. Many people have walked these paths before you. There have been many, many people who didn't fall into society's picture-perfect image and are doing amazing, life-sized things right now. You need to study the other teens who have believed the same lies that you've been told. Find the people in your school, your community, or on social media who are living life on their own terms. It's likely they were told the exact same lies and worked hard to overcome their beliefs. They're not letting anyone or anything hold them back. Absorb all their good vibes and realize that they're not letting societal expectations hold them back, and neither should you.

Stop Believing Lies Tip #3

Some of the lies we believe are not all created from societal expectations. Sadly, some of them we create ourselves. We tell ourselves hurtful things like "I need to make everyone happy" or "I don't get along well with other people." Both of those statements are untrue and unfair. You absolutely don't need to make everyone happy. It would be nearly impossible. And you probably get along with others just fine. If you're not getting along with others, there's likely a specific reason why. It's not because you just flat out don't get along with people. So my advice to you is to identify the lies that you're telling yourself. Find the root of the lie. Did someone else plant the seed many years ago? (Like my friend accidentally did in ping pong.) Or is this a lie you created yourself because you lacked confidence in your abilities? Additional steps can be taken, but first, identify the lies and find the root.

Stop Believing Lies Tip #4

If you continue to believe the lies that are creating barriers around your life, go back and read chapter 5 again. Maybe you need to be more consistent with your positive affirmations. Maybe you need to write a list of strengths next to the lies you believe about yourself. Boosting your self-confidence will help to overcome this negativity. The more consistent you are with affirmations, the farther away you'll get from the lies.

Chapter 12
Diversity's Going to
Change Your Life

When I first started writing this chapter, I googled the definition of "diversity" and the answer that came up said "the state of being diverse."

I couldn't help but laugh and mumble "Thanks, Google" under my breath. That answer alone gave me enough motivation to continue writing this chapter because I feel like that's what many teens will understand about the word. They'll read the definition, giggle like I did, and move onto researching something else.

I'm sure you've heard of the word diversity before, but just in case, the Merriam Webster definition did a much better job, and it looks more like this:

DIVERSITY: the condition of having or being composed of differing elements: VARIETY
especially: the inclusion of people from different races, cultures, etc. in a group or organization

That definition definitely did a better job and I especially like the focus on the second part. *The inclusion of people from different races, cultures, etc.*

Now, having read that, I want you to think of your circle. I know I already mentioned that phrase "you are the five people you surround yourself with the most" but I want you to think about it again.

And no, it doesn't count if you hang out with a lot of animals or have seventeen cats. I'm not counting it.

I want you to think about the people you spend the most time with. Do you have a circle of friends? Is it a big group or a small group? Is it your family or your siblings? Is it your peers that you see at school or is it a community you met online? Is it a religious group or maybe a volunteer club in your neighborhood?

Regardless of how you know these people, it's important to know how much time you spend with them. Because whoever these people are that you spend the most time with, know that you're a combination of them. The people around you influence your behaviors so much that you might start to act like them, talk like them, walk like them, eat like them, etc.

You are a combination of the people around you, and it's my instinct that you surround yourself with people who are very similar to you. It's likely that you and your friends have similar interests, similar beliefs, and similar tendencies. You guys might even dress alike, talk alike, and for heaven's sake, you probably even look alike.

If that's true, then this chapter might change your life. And if it is true, don't blame yourself. It's not your fault. It's our human instinct to connect with likeminded people. We want to surround ourselves with people who make us feel comfortable and accepted.

It's also possible that you've never had the opportunity to diversify your friendships. Shoot, you might also know nothing about diversity, or maybe you've been taught to avoid it altogether. I don't know what your thing is, but I know I want to change the pattern.

Maya Angelou—famous American poet, civil rights activist, and you've probably read some of her works in school before—said, "It is time for parents to teach young people early on that in diversity there is beauty and there is strength."

I am totally with my girl Maya here because diversity makes us stronger. It makes us knowledgeable. It allows us to be empathetic and compassionate. Teens should not only surround themselves with people who are similar to them but also with people who are nothing like them at all. Diversity is a key to growth and being the best possible version of you.

We've already talked about identity in chapter 8, and like I said then, many teens are uncomfortable with their identity. It's likely because they aren't being true to their authentic self. Teens often feel pressured to succumb to the tendencies and people they're constantly surrounded by. Sometimes, the people around us are *not* the best people for our soul. Sometimes, we remain friends with people simply because we've known them for so long, but deep down, you've grown into two totally different people. Sometimes, we continue to be friends with people because it's comfortable and the thought of making new friends seems uncomfortable and childish.

But, let me ask you this: if you were surrounded by people who inspire you, people you admire, people with a growth mindset, don't you think your identity would be clearer? You'd be able to identify as an optimistic person, someone with inspiring friends, and everything wouldn't be so confusing.

We need people in our circle who breathe life into us. We need people who are kind, caring, and compassionate. We need people who will encourage us and challenge us to push through and get through the hard days. We need people who have our back and remind us of our worth, our value, our love, our strength, our power as an individual. If you don't have someone to do that, then this chapter is for you.

This chapter is focused on diversifying your life, your friendships, your surroundings, your overall everyday portfolio. Teens need diversity because it brings in new ideas and new experiences. You can learn about other cultures and better understand the world around you. Diversity expands your communication skills, your overall dialogue, and it boosts creativity. Embracing the significance of diversity is going to change your life.

Look at Your Circle

Be honest with yourself when you look at the circle of people you spend the most time with. You are a combination of those people. It's just how it works. When we spend so much time with people, we tend to pick up their tendencies. If you spend time with friends who love to play sports, you're likely an athlete. If you spend time with friends who like to skateboard, you're likely a skateboarder. If you spend time with friends who are artists, you're likely an artist. If you spend time with friends who are musicians, you're likely a musician.

Do you guys see what I'm doing here?

Good.

With that said, look at your circle of friends again. Do you honestly want to be a combination of them? If your answer is *yes*, then that's amazing! Maybe you have a diverse group of friends who are amazing and creative and inspiring and breathe life into you.

But if your answer is *no*, then you might be limiting yourself by only spending time with those people. I would never tell you to end your friendships and I'm definitely not saying that now. I'm just opening you up to the idea that there's room for *more* friends. You have the power to make *new* friends and bring *more* people into your current circle. Practice the art of diversifying your current circle and bring new people with new faces, new knowledge, new jokes, new everything. New friendships could change your life.

Don't be one of those teens who think "I have all the friends I need. No more room on this bandwagon." If you are that person, I'm being blunt here but I promise, you're limiting yourself. Get used to the idea of having more friends, new friends, and diverse friends. Like our girl Maya said, within diversity, there is beauty and there is strength.

Sometimes, when we're surrounded by the same people all too often, habits begin to form. Maybe you develop the same habits that they have. Maybe your circle of friends uses the same language and says the same phrases. Maybe your circle dresses similarly, walks similarly, and uses the same type of body language. You already know that your subconscious mind records your daily activities and stores it as information in the brain. This will eventually become a habit and your identity is influenced by the people you're surrounded by. Ask yourself this question: are you doing things subconsciously when you're with your friends?

If the answer is *yes*, then don't worry. It happens to most of us—teens and adults alike. But now you know how powerful it is to have a plethora of different people in your circle. These people will influence your thoughts, your actions, your behaviors, your habits, your future, and the way you feel about yourself.

Now that you've opened up to the idea of making new friends, you might be curious as to how you can do that. In all honesty, I know making new friends as a teen isn't always easy. How do you just magically become friends with someone? It's not like kindergarten when you just walked up to someone and said, "Do you want to be my friend?" If only it were that simple. But I understand that it's not. So let's dive into some ideas on how you can make new friends.

Gap Years Are the Bomb

You want to learn how to be more diverse? Traveling is going to make you the most diverse dang teen in the world.

I mentioned earlier that I've backpacked through a zillion and a half countries (just kidding, it wasn't that many), but I'm so in love with traveling that I wouldn't be doing you justice if I didn't write a section in here about it.

When I was a teen, doing vocational school or gap year programs seemed like a taboo thing to do. I don't remember anyone offering them to me and making it seem like a great, plausible option. Not to mention, anytime school trips came up or any type of travel experience, it always seemed way too expensive and way out of my family's budget.

Well, kid, I'm here to tell you what I've learned so that you have more opportunities than I did.

Vocational school is not taboo. It's actually brilliant. They teach you real life skills that will be super meaningful in your life, long after your teen years have ended.

Gap year programs are also not taboo. In fact, they're the freaking bomb. And they might not be nearly as expensive as you think either.

Many teens (including my former self) have absolutely no idea what they want to do after high school. I mean, how in the world are you supposed to know what you want to go to college for? If you do, that's pretty cool. But if you don't, doing a gap year program or going to vocational school might be great options for you.

If you've never heard of a gap year before, well, it's exactly what it sounds like. You take a year-long break from your education to explore some new opportunities and see what sparks your interest. I'm 28 years old and I've taken a few gap years and I intend on taking many, many more in my future. So trust me, they are worth it.

Alexa Gonzalez, MSEd, high school guidance counselor, and my second super awesome sister-in-law, says, "Burnout after high school is real. While some young people reach graduation energized to face what's next, most are crawling over the finish line, exhausted and uninspired. A gap year can give you the time, space, and freedom to breathe, reflect, and explore. Think of it as a gift to yourself—the gift of time to find your inner compass."

You can do a national program where you stay in your home country and work on development activities and learn different types of work. Or you can do an international program, go abroad, see the world, and do fun activities. You'll likely volunteer and learn other types of work.

You can go to Costa Rica and learn about the environment; you can go to London and learn about business; you could work with wildlife in South Africa; you could spend a semester on a boat and sail from the Caribbean to Tahiti; you could learn marine conservation and support the coral reefs in Fiji or Thailand. There are a million different programs that you could explore and pick the ones that work best for you. There are also people around the world (counselors if you will) who will help you design a series of trips—one that's tailored to you and helps to fit your budget. All you have to do is go online and do some research. After making your bucket list, I can only imagine there might be a few places you'd love to visit.

These gap year programs and vocational schools will not only diversify your portfolio and educate you on new things you haven't learned yet but it will also be the perfect chance to meet new people. My instinct is that the teens who are open to different programs and trying new things will be fun, exciting, interesting people to connect with. They'll probably love the idea of making new friends and will likely be easy to talk to.

If traveling isn't an option for you, what about a part-time job? Or a volunteer experience? I know I've said this a zillion times already, but the more experiences you have, the more chances you'll have to meet new people and make new friends.

Get active in your community. I'm sure there are a number of clubs or youth group programs you can join. Most communities have environmental groups like Habitat for Humanity or Key Club. I'm sure there are a variety of leagues you could join like softball, soccer, basketball, etc. If you don't like intense sports, I'm fairly confident there's a yoga studio and meditation center somewhere close to you. You can do any type of music club, art club, or scouting program.

The reality is there's a ton of things you can do to meet new friends and diversify your portfolio. All you have to do is be willing to give it a try. If you're not willing to try, you'll never know what connections you might be missing out on.

Your Time Is Coming, My Friend

I'll be flat out honest here when I say this: high school isn't the best time for everyone. I admitted that in the beginning of the book for me. It really wasn't.

Most teens grow up having this image that high school is supposed to be amazing and fun; and when you look around at everyone else, it seems like everyone has friends, good looks, athleticism, and everything all figured out.

The reality is that *none* of you have it figured out.

There it is. I said it. It might've been like a smack in the face (I hope not!). But it's the truth! How could you possibly have it figured out? When you're in high school, you're limited by the people in your school or your community. And if you're anything like me and you come from a small town, then there just might not be a lot of people to connect with. If that's the case, it's totally normal and it happens to a lot of teens around the world.

Many of you feel like you're in the wrong circle because you don't truly connect with those people. Honestly, I was there too. I had a few friends in high school, but I never felt like we really connected on the level I was hoping for. Well, I ended up finding my circle after high school, after college, through a new friend who I worked with.

My advice to you is to stay hopeful. Your time is coming. Outside of your school, there are millions of teens around the world who would love to connect with you. They, too, simply haven't met you yet.

The difference between you and I is that you have a book filled with tips and tricks that I didn't know until my teen years ended. You are brighter, more knowledgeable, and stronger than you know possible. Use these tips to help diversify your life. I wish I knew them when I was a teen because I would have loved a range of diversity teaching me new things about the world.

I promise you will make new friends and you'll have laughs and good times and lots of memories for a lifetime. Go back to chapter 6 and visualize these friends if you have to. Your time is coming, my friend, so stay hopeful.

Diversity Tip #1

Most adults become friends with the people they work with. Getting a job might not sound like the most exciting thing to you, but I promise, it's where most of my best relationships have been formed. Look for a summer job. A camp counselor or at an ice cream parlor maybe?

Somewhere that's fun and relaxing and somewhere that other teens will be. If teens are there, conversations will naturally strike up and you'll gladly be able to meet new people.

Diversity Tip #2

Maybe you already know someone who you'd like to be friends with. Maybe you just haven't been able to connect with that person yet. I say, stop waiting for the perfect time. Be confident. Walk up to the person and strike up a conversation. Ask if you can have lunch with them. It doesn't have to be anything crazy. People love being complimented, so you could say something like this: "Hey! You look like a lot of fun and I could use some of your energy! Would you mind if we got lunch today?" I'm sure anyone would love to get a compliment like that and I'm sure that answer would be an easy "YES!"

Diversity Tip #3

Talk to old people. Haha! Yes, I did just say that. Old people are notorious for saying things like "when I was your age..." And it might cause you to roll your eyes or giggle under your breath. Regardless, there's meaning to it. Older people like to share stories about their experiences. Listen to their stories, ask questions, find out how they built the connections they have today. Their stories might inspire you to try the same experiences, diversify your portfolio, and meet new friends along the way.

Diversity Tip #4

Talk to a counselor. It's likely you have a counselor at your school who would love to help you dabble in new experiences, try new things, and make new friends. If you're looking for something specific, tell them what you want. Let them provide you with opportunities and go from there.

Chapter 13
Sometimes, Adults Don't Get It

Have you ever been super annoyed with just about every adult in your life? If you have, I hear you and I relate to that. I remember some days going to school and being frustrated with my teachers and then coming home to be frustrated with my parents. On those days, I felt isolated and alone. *I felt like adults just didn't get it.*

Most of the time, adults are great and probably want what's best for you. But sometimes, adults just don't get it. I'm in this weird phase where I remember my teens years but I also understand why adults say most of the things they say.

Adults have experienced many of the same things that you're going through. We know that you're going to make it through these tough teen years so we try to give you advice and tell you how to get through it. Adults will share their experiences and let you know how they handled it. We tell you to learn from our mistakes. The thing is, sometimes, you don't need our advice. Sometimes, you just need to experience the thing in order to learn from it—just like we did.

An expert is someone with authoritative knowledge or skill in a particular area. Something happens when you become an adult that you feel like you've mastered your teen years. Adults feel as if they've survived those tough times and their survival means expertise. The truth is, most adults aren't experts at all. You guys are the ones going through your teen years in today's world, today's society, with all the knowledge that today brings. *You, my friend, are the expert.*

Every new generation is going to bring so much diversity, so much information, that it's you teens who should be teaching us. You guys are so open to changing our society and being more compassionate, more civil, more caring people. You guys are the ones who get it, not the adults. In many ways, we're a little outdated and a little out of touch when it comes to being a teen.

Knowing that you are the true expert, take your role seriously. Be graceful with the adults in your life and try to educate them on what it's like to be a teen today. We are *constantly* learning from you.

In this chapter, we're going to dive into the fact that adults aren't always right and how to handle your emotions when adults upset you. We're also going to talk about why you shouldn't be in such a hurry to become an adult, because just like teens, adults make mistakes too. We're all trying to figure out this thing called life—children, teens, and adults alike. We're all on this journey together.

Why Are You Trying to Be an Adult?

This whole chapter is focusing on how adults make mistakes too. So why are so many of you teens trying to grow up so fast? I'm sure a lot of it has to do with social media comparisons and trying to keep up with your peers, but my gosh, you guys. Some of you are 13 going on 30. It's crazy!

Many of you teens are so mature and smart and talented. Some of you are so stinkin' good at putting makeup on. (A lot better than me, that's for sure!) You guys are beautiful, witty, and really fun to hang out with. I certainly don't remember being as cool as you when I was a teen.

When I was younger, I was dirty and sweaty and running around like a hot mess. I had acne and was overweight and I was cheesy and nerdy and all over the place.

Something happened over the last decade because now, I feel like you guys jump right over that awkward phase. You go from middle school right into adulthood. Of course, I want you to be comfortable in your own skin, so if jumping from one phase to the next is your thing and you want to do that, then go for it. But don't be scared to stay a teen a little bit longer too.

I wish I could make the time slow down because I know you're going to miss some of these teen years. When you get to adulthood, you're going to realize that you're still just as clueless as you were when you were a teen. Adults are just like you and we're learning new things every day. We're figuring out how to navigate life too, so if you can slow down, I think you'll be grateful for it.

As soon as you turn 20, just like that, those teen years are over. And sure, it's exciting, but it's also a little sad too. So be a teen, my friend, and enjoy it while it lasts. There's no reason to rush into adulthood because it's going to happen no matter what. Remember we said that growth is inevitable? I promise you it's true. You will grow into an adult when the right time comes, so try to stay a teen a little bit longer.

Adults Say the Wrong Things Too

Remember in chapter 2 when we talked about being a better listener? It really is such an important tool that will enhance your relationships with everyone.

Why?

Well, the answer is simple. Because everyone wants to be heard.

Unfortunately, not all adults master the art of listening in their teen years. And just like everyone else, adults want to be heard too. The reality is that adults say the wrong things sometimes.

Just because we're a little older doesn't mean we can't make mistakes. Most of the adults in your life have likely not been taught how to be a great listener. Help them to learn.

Be specific about what you're looking for in a listener. At times when you're seeking advice, ask for it. Other times when you just want someone to listen to your problems, tell them that. The more specific you are, the better the listener they will be. This clarification will help prevent adults from accidently saying the wrong things.

This section is short, but it's easy. Always remember that adults make mistakes too. We are growing in this world, just like you are. Tomorrow is a day that neither you nor I nor your parents nor any other adult on Earth has ever lived through before. We should attempt to ascertain tomorrow together.

So even when adults make mistakes, give them grace. Be patient and understanding because sometimes, adults say the wrong things too.

Stop Counting Down

Most adults in today's world are in a countdown. They count down the years until they can retire from their jobs. They count down the days until they go on vacation. They count down the minutes until they can leave work and go home. Then, they get home and they count down the minutes until the kids go to sleep and they can sit down and watch TV. Adults are constantly counting down the times until they can move on to something they consider to be better than what they're currently doing.

This is a horrible habit that adults desperately need to change, and I'm here to tell you to stop following their footsteps. Don't go to school and count down every second until the bell rings. Don't go to practice and count down the minutes until you can walk off the field. Enjoy the precious minutes you have because I promise they're going to fly.

If you adopt this habit of counting down now, while you're in your teens, then it's going to follow you into adulthood. By counting down your seconds, minutes, hours, and days, you're essentially wasting your life. You're constantly trying to move on to the next thing without appreciating the smaller moments in life.

As a teen, you have the rest of your life to do anything, be anything, think about anything. A teen should not be focused on counting down their days until they become an adult. Because then, as an adult, you begin counting down your days until you grow old. And then, from there, you simply count down your days. It's sad, honestly. And I'm here to help change that narrative for you.

Enjoy your days. Enjoy the little minutes that don't seem like a big deal. Look forward to the next thing with excitement but don't jump ahead too fast. You'll get there when you get there and it'll be the perfect timing. Stop limiting yourself and counting your days because they're going to count down for you, there's no reason to keep track.

The moral of this section is to stop following in the footsteps of adults who are constantly counting down their days and always onto the next thing. It's likely they haven't mastered the skill of being in the moment and they haven't appreciated time for the magical and fascinating tool that it is. Life seems long, kid, but it's too short to count. So I say, make more memories and count those instead.

"Work Harder," They Say

In addition to counting down, many adults live in a state of chaos. I hope your parents, guardians, teachers, or any other adult in your life doesn't read this and get offended by that statement, but honestly, it's the truth.

It's not necessarily their fault though, it's the way our society has been molded. With that said, most adults in our culture work their tails off because they feel obligated to work unbelievably hard. We've been pressured since we were little to have resilience, persevere, and make others proud. We feel as if we must achieve success, though many of us don't even know how we would even define success if we had to.

Most of our jobs invite us to work long hours and we feel like a burden when we need to take time for ourselves. Our society encourages adults to push harder and we are living in a go-go-go type of mentality.

As a result of this, many adults do not take the rest and relaxation that they need in order to keep showing up every day at a high-intensity level. It results in a constant state of chaos.

Kid, do me a favor and avoid this. Do not fall into this trap. I do not believe it is OK to continually live in a state of chaos.

You should not always feel pressured to work harder, run faster, and be better day in and day out. Some seasons of your life might be busy and productive, but others might look more zen and quiet. You don't always have to feel like you're pushing so hard. You don't always have to feel like you're in a full-on sprint. Give yourself the chance to breathe.

If you have adults in your life who are always in that chaotic state, it's likely that they are brilliantly hard-workers. I imagine they are dedicated and diligent. My instinct is that they are strong, driven, and powerful individuals. However, as amazing as I'm sure they are, you already know that sometimes, adults make mistakes too. It's possible they aren't giving themselves the self-care that their body needs. Don't follow into the trap of chaos. Follow your body, give yourself a chance to breathe, and know when it's relaxation season. Your generation has the power to change these societal expectations of always working harder. Be the change our world needs to see.

The Power of the Unsent Letter

In this section, we're going to talk about abstract concepts so I'll start by telling you what in the world that even is.

An abstract concept is an idea that takes no physical form. They are intangible thoughts that you can't physically touch, which is the opposite of concrete objects, or something with tangible elements that you can physically touch. A few examples of abstract concepts include freedom, love, friendship, ego, and anxiety. Basically anything that ends with *ism* is also an abstract concept: feminism, racism, communism, and nationalism are all examples of abstract concepts. You know they exist, but you can't physically touch them.

As I mentioned in the beginning of the chapter, sometimes, adults just don't get it. Sometimes, they make you angry or upset or confused. Sometimes, you feel like your voice isn't being heard and the adults around you aren't listening.

At those times, there's a simple thing you could do to help feel heard and get your feelings out. It's called the unsent letter.

Pick an abstract concept that you want to address. Maybe it's an emotion, a diagnosis, a specific relationship that you want to address. Once you've picked it, you're going to write a letter to it. Let's say the abstract concept you've picked is anger. Your letter is going to say, *"Dear Anger..."*

Then write an entire letter talking to anger as if it took human form. You're addressing anger and stating what it does to you. Ask anger if he or she will be around forever. Ask questions, explain how anger makes you feel, and talk as if you're actually going to send the letter.

At the end, read through it. Reflect on it. Marinate your thoughts, your emotions, your ideas. I'll bet you'll feel a hundred times better just for getting the thoughts out of your brain and down on paper.

The amazing thing about this is that you never actually have to send the letter. In fact, go ahead and throw that letter out. Rip it up. Toss it in the garbage and get rid of the anger that you feel.

When you're feeling flooded with emotions, your emotions have the best of you. They're controlling you. But when you write the letter, you take back control. You're getting all of the anger out and then you're literally throwing it away. No more anger. It's brilliant actually and I highly recommend you do this.

So, let's take a few minutes to pause and I'll let you give the unsent letter a try. Think of an abstract concept that you'd like to address. It doesn't have to be negative if you don't feel negative emotions either. Maybe you're feeling optimistic toward something (love, success, freedom, education, etc.). But it's up to you. You pick! Then go below and write your letter. Write as much as you possibly can and write like no one's watching. In fact, no one is watching so go ahead, kid! Get your thoughts onto paper.

The Unsent Letter:

That was fun, wasn't it? The unsent letter is amazing so I hope you've enjoyed it as much as I do. This tool will come in handy time and time again when you're flooded with emotions. It'll come in handy when adults aren't listening to you and you feel like you need to get your thoughts out. Sometimes, you don't want an adult to solve your problems. Sometimes, you just want them to hear you and know what you're feeling. In those times, write the letter.

What's cool about this concept too is that it doesn't always have to be written to an abstract concept. I like doing that to become aware of our emotions and identify what feelings are controlling us. But honestly, you can write the letter to anyone or anything that you want.

If you're feeling upset with your parents or friends or teachers or siblings or your baseball team, your high school, the community you live in, it doesn't matter. Just write the letter and get everything out. When you go back and read the letter, you can pull out the most important pieces of information. Then you can go to that person and explain to them (with composure) how you're feeling. It probably won't be a heightened conversation because you've already gotten your heaviest feelings out on paper and the letter helped you to navigate your thoughts and pull out what topics are most important.

This tool will be valuable for the rest of your life. In fact, I'm an adult and I still use it today. So I hope you enjoyed it. If you do, keep using it. It's quick, it's easy, and it's a way you can help manage your own emotions without the help of an adult.

Adults Don't Get It Tip #1

Even though adults may seem difficult at times, most of them are really trying to do the right thing. They're trying to help you navigate your teen years. They're trying to keep you safe, keep you young, and keep you innocent. They want to help. My advice to you is to give them grace. Be kind and understanding. Develop positive relationships with the adults in your life because they can make the hard times a little easier. Plus, I'm sure they do have great advice when you're ready to receive it.

Adults Don't Get It Tip #2

I'm sure there's an adult in your life who might seem a little more in tune with their teen self. If that's true, ask them for mentorship. I'm sure they'd love to mentor you and help you to navigate your teen years. If you adapt the unsent letter strategy, you can even share your letters with that mentor. Having one adult in your life who understands your emotions and what you're going through can make a significant difference. You don't need all the adults to understand. Just seek out one.

Chapter 14
This Too Shall Pass

This is an amazing phrase that I'm sure you've heard a time or two before. Even Honest Abe himself used this phrase in his speeches. And yes, for those of you who are wondering, I do like Teddy Roosevelt and all, but Abraham Lincoln is definitely my favorite president. He just seemed so cool, so down to earth, he sought justice, and was super humble. He was quite the guy, and when I saw that he used the phrase "This too shall pass" in his speeches, well, it made me love him all the more. The phrase has been widely used over many, many years and translated into various languages around the world.

You: But Nicole, what the heck does it mean?
Me: Great question, kid! Let's keep going…

The phrase is quite simple to break down and it focuses on something we've already talked about: change. Change is the evolution of growth. Our lives are constantly in motion and we are constantly changing. We are forever evolving. Day by day, minute by minute, second by second, you will never be as young as you are right now. By the time you reach the end of this chapter, you will have experienced growth again, because you'll have new knowledge that you didn't have before. And by tomorrow, you'll experience growth again because you have never lived through whatever tomorrow brings. And that will continue to happen for the rest of your life. It's a pretty wild thing to think about.

If you want even more proof, here's another weird fact to think about: your body fully regenerates itself every seven years. All new cells. A completely different person. Every seven years. It's mind blowing. Talk about change! You literally change into a whole new person every seven years. So next time you think you can't do something, think again! If you can change into a completely new version of yourself every seven years, you can do absolutely anything!

So, getting back to the phrase, *this too shall pass* means that nothing lasts forever. Whether it's good or bad, it doesn't last forever. When something is good, appreciate it. Be aware and present and open to the good things because they won't last forever. When something is bad, it's easier to manage the pain when you know that it won't last forever.

If I understood this phase in high school, I think I would have been able to understand the world around me a bit better than I *actually* did. And if this manuscript allowed it, I'd definitely add an eyeroll emoji at the end of that sentence. Maybe the crying-laughing one too.

The reason is because I *thought* I knew the world around me. Really, I thought I did. But I was very wrong. In fact, I was pretty naive because when we're teens, we only get to see the world from our family's eyes. We live in a house with our parents, sometimes other siblings, and everyone in your house has the ability to impact you—both positively and negatively. Thus, it makes it really hard to understand the world when you're living in a house with the same people you've known your whole life.

This phrase helps you to step outside of your own shoes and see the world from a different view. That is what this chapter is all about: seeing the world from a different perspective, and I'm hoping to show you how. At the end of this chapter, I hope you have a slightly new outlook on your life. I want you to see the world through the lens of your absolute best self.

Time for Another Throwback

This throwback is going to be a bit different than the last one. Instead of looking back on your own life, I want you to look back in history. Look back in American history, European history, African history, Asian history, etc. Look back in the history of all of mankind. If you're pretty well-versed in history, then you'll know that we've been through some pretty crazy things.

As a human race, we've been through imperialism, genocides, diseases and other widespread viruses. We've survived hundreds, if not thousands of wars—one of them involving nuclear power. We've survived population booms, agricultural crises, stock market crashes, and economic failures. We've survived severe natural disasters, horrible leaders, and some good leaders too. We've seen leaders assassinated more times than I'd like to count. We've seen new movements form and people gather around the globe to support worldwide protests. We've lived through industrialization and new advancements in technology. We've seen people come together more times than they've failed.

I could add about a zillion more things to that list because mankind has been around for roughly 300,000 years! That's a long time, you guys, and although we've suffered through various traumatic experiences, we've also done some really cool things.

However, on that same note, we've hardly scratched the surface. Earth has been a planet for roughly 4.5 billion years.

When you look at those numbers, it actually feels like mankind hasn't been on Earth for very long at all. For heaven's sake there were giant dinosaurs walking around our planet 65 million years before we humans even became a thing! It's so insanely wild to think about.

And yet, it happened.

So, on a broad scale, I want you to look at Earth as if you were standing in space. Look at all of it from a big picture. Stop looking at Earth like you're standing in your bedroom. You can't see everything from there because your vision is clouded by the walls, the curtains, and all the other things blocking your view. You need to take a million steps outward and look at it from a broader perspective. Once you do, you'll understand the meaning of *this too shall pass*.

Dinosaurs lived a really cool life, but eventually their time came to an end. And just like that, 65 million years passed in the blink of an eye, and humans appeared on Earth. And we've lived through some pretty crazy things, but eventually, all of those crazy things have come to an end. Our wars have ended, our heartaches have ended, our journey to the moon has ended, all the natural disasters have ended, all global pandemics have ended, and we've continued on. We *always* continue on.

Once you can look at the world from a broad view, a view outside of your own bubble, you'll recognize that we always press on. It's what we do. We're humans and we're really freaking tough creatures. Everything in life will come to pass, and we will always march on.

Multiple Personalities Come up Again

In chapter 8, we talked about having multiple personalities and how different people trigger different behaviors. Now that we're aware of this and you know these multiple personalities are totally normal, we're going to take it a step further and talk about how they can really come in handy.

Teens don't always believe that good things should happen for them. It's an awful truth that we desperately need to fix and it's a result of low confidence and a lack of self-love. Sometimes, when bad things happen, teens convince themselves that they deserved it. Well, I'm here to tell you that you don't deserve anything bad to happen to you. You never have and you never will. I promise you that. No one deserves bad things to happen.

At the same time, it's true that everyone's going to have hard days in their life. It's inevitable because we're not living in a fantasy world where we're surrounded by rainbows and purple trees and where everyone looks like a marshmallow. That does sound cool but this is the real world and difficult days happen.

And during those hard seasons, I want you to encourage your toughest self to surface. You already know that you have multiple personalities so why don't you acknowledge them? Identify them. Give them a name if you'd like. Maybe your tough personality is The Hulk and your chill, relaxing personality is Marley. I don't know, you pick the names. But when the time comes and you need your toughest, strongest, baddest self to surface, then call out The Hulk.

It doesn't have to be super cheesy either. It's just a tactic for your brain so that you can easily flip the switch and have the right mindset you need to get through the thing you need to get through. When teens are struggling to be mentally tough, it's usually because they don't have the right mindset to embrace whatever it is that they're going through.

And that's not on you, kid. I've mentioned this before and I'll say it a million times more if I have to, but I think our education model needs an upgrade. I believe developing a positive mindset, learning optimism, growth, and self-love are some of the most important tools you'll ever discover. We should be teaching it as a required class in school.

Nonetheless, now that you have this book, you know the secrets and strategies to build your positive mindset and develop into the best possible version of you. So from here on out, it *is* on you. Take the knowledge you're learning here and implement it into your life.

This is just one more tool to add to your toolbox. Separate the multiple identities that you have. Reflect on the personality that's gotten you through some of the hard times that you've experienced. Give that person a name and know that version of you as the person who's going to take on all the hard things for years to come. Next time something does come up, that side of you will be able to surface. That side of you will not only say "This too shall pass" but they'll say "I find meaning in everything that happens and this too shall pass quicker than ever so I can go back to relaxing with Marley."

Cheesy, I know, but you get the point!

Setbacks Are Setups

Being rejected sucks. It really does. It hurts and it basically tells us that we're not worthy or we're not the perfect fit. It points out our imperfections and makes us feel small. I'm here to tell you there's something exciting about being rejected though. It's so exciting that it might make you look forward to hearing the word "no" or getting rejected. (OK, maybe not all the time, but it'll certainly make rejection a lot easier to process!)

Truth is, we all experience rejection. When you're a teen, it happens a lot. You go through break ups and heartaches. Your friends might make new friends and drift apart from you. You apply to colleges and might not get into all of them. Whatever the rejection is, it really does hurt and if you've experienced this before, then you know exactly what I'm talking about.

Well, guess what, kid!

I can finally tell you through growth and experience that those painful setbacks are *actually* setups. Your rejection is secretly a blessing in disguise because it's going to set you up for something even greater in the future. You'll only know this for certain if you keep pushing forward, and when you do, you'll learn exactly why you were rejected. It's likely you were meant to go down a different path and you'll say, "Wow, I really dodged a bullet with that setback."

When you are feeling hurt because of rejection or any type of failure, know that there is meaning to the rejection. There's a purpose for it that you haven't learned about yet. The rejection is actually preparing you for something better that hasn't surfaced yet. It hasn't come into your path *yet,* and that's so exciting to think about! To know that something amazing lies ahead of you, but you don't know what it is. It's like waiting for your birthday—you know you're going to have some gifts to open but you have no idea what they are! The anticipation is probably wild, but it's so exciting at the same time.

We're going to talk more about the word *yet* in chapter 15 because it's one of the most important words you'll learn in your teen years. The word yet has infinite power to it. It reminds you that great things are coming.

So, always remember that setbacks are really setups for something amazing. Setbacks make you stronger even when you don't realize it. Some of you might be experiencing rejection right now and you may feel hurt or weak, but it's a sign that you're growing and you don't even know it. That weakness reflects your body getting stronger.

You: *But Nicole, that doesn't make any sense.*
Me: *OK, OK, let me explain a little differently.*

Have you ever gone to the gym and felt sore afterwards? Maybe you're on a sports team and your coach makes you run sprints up and down the field. Maybe you've gone to a yoga class before. Regardless of the activity, if you've ever exercised, you know what I'm talking about. You were probably sore the next day.

That soreness doesn't mean you did a bad thing. Your body is physically in pain because you pushed your muscles a little harder than they're used to and they're recovering from the intensity. That is literally your body's way of getting stronger and repairing itself. It's a beautiful thing because it shows you that to get stronger, you're going to feel a little pain.

Your mindset works the same way your muscles do. When you experience any type of setback, you're going to feel hurt or rejected. That pain is your mind's way of recovering from the setback. And once you get past it, the pain disappears, you grow mentally stronger, and you continue on your path to something greater. How beautiful is that?

I think it's pretty stinkin' cool. So, now, when anyone tells you "no," remember to smile because that rejection is a part of your journey to something better. It's going to make you wiser and stronger, and it's going to be the best setup you'll ever have because in the future there's something so much greater for you—something so much better than the path you *thought* you were going to go down. That first one was simply not the path that you were meant to be on.

If someone broke up with you, in the future you'll have a partner who's going to be more compatible and who will love you for who you are as a person. If you get rejected from a college that you thought you were going to attend, well, guess what? Future you will attend another university, one that's so much better suited for you, and you're going to have an amazing experience there. Why? Because setbacks are the most amazing setups you could possibly imagine.

Always keep in mind that the pain will pass, just like all types of pain does. Physical pain, emotional pain, mental pain, they all run their course and allow you to grow into a stronger, brighter version of you.

When you're feeling overwhelmed by emotions or like no one's listening to you, remember *this too shall pass*. When you feel anxious or depressed or tired or scared, remember *this too shall pass*. When someone tells you something you don't want to hear, remember *this too shall pass*. When you experience grief, or loss, or heartache, or rejection, remember *this too shall pass*. When your parents aren't letting you do what you want to do, remember *this too shall pass*.

Next time you're feeling any type of negative emotion, always remember that it will pass. These years will pass. Just like everything in the world, they will pass. And it seems like the moment your teen years come to pass, everything else begins to fly. And during this journey, always remember that your setbacks are your setups secretly guiding you to the amazing path that you're meant to be on.

This Too Shall Pass Tip #1

The reason I wrote this book is because I know that your teen years can be some of the most physically and emotionally stressful years of your life. For some, it will be.

For others, it won't. But for you, I want you to have the choice. If you don't want to experience high levels of stress and pain, you don't have to. You can go through these years with the knowledge and understanding that these years will pass. Constant reminders will help you to go through your days knowing that these years don't have to be so stressful. Set a daily reminder on your phone in the middle of the day saying *This too shall pass*. On some days, you might not need the reminder. On other days, when you're going through a moment of pain, this reminder will pop up and you'll be able to smile because you'll know this feeling of rejection, or hurt, or heartache, or whatever negative emotion you're feeling, it will pass.

This Too Shall Pass Tip #2

Sometimes, we get so wrapped up in negative emotions because we're worried about what other people will think. My best piece of advice is to follow your intuition. Always go with your gut feeling and it will likely help you to get past the hard thing you're going through. You teens were created with this amazing thing called intuition for a reason, and it allows you to subconsciously make decisions without analytical reasoning. That's pretty freaking cool. It's almost like a superpower. Sometimes, teens are stuck in negative emotions because they're concerned about the opinions of their parents, peers, or siblings. I say, follow your intuition because your gut knows the meaning of the world, and it understands that *this too shall pass*.

This Too Shall Pass Tip #3

There are other people who have overcome the same hard things that you're struggling to overcome. Find those people! You need to seek them out. You can look in your school or in your community. If they're not local, then search them online. If you're struggling through a hard season, go online and research people who have dealt with the same traumas. I'm almost positive there's an online community waiting to connect with you. If there isn't, I'm still confident that someone else's story is online for you to read. Study those people. Learn from them. Sometimes, just hearing that other people have walked through the same paths as you can be a helpful reminder that you're not alone. You can also find that person on social media. Ask for support and build a connection with them. Every time you go on social media, your news feed will display their good vibes as a reminder that you can overcome any struggle.

Chapter 15
You're Freaking Amazing

I saved this chapter for last because it's probably the most important topic in the entire book. If I know you like I think I do, it's likely that you've had some moments of doubt in your life. Sometimes, you second guess your choices and you lack confidence in yourself.

I know you have these feelings because in high school, you already know, but I felt the same way. I remember having low self-confidence and yet, it seemed like most people didn't care. I went to school every day to learn math equations and biology, but never once did I learn about self-love. I didn't learn about positive affirmations and how to build my morale. Thankfully, I made it through my teen years and learned about personal development after high school. But I'm here to change that narrative for you. I want you to discover the magic of personal growth at an early age and have the best teens years you could possibly imagine.

By the time you've picked up this book and started reading it, I'm sure you've endured some hard things. Even though we're all on separate journeys, we all experience difficult seasons in life. Some of you may have survived through your parents' divorce or the death of a loved one. Some of you may have lost a pet or had to change schools. Some of you may not have a lot of friends or any friends at all. Some of you may have a diagnosis or anxiety or an overall poor self-image. Whatever it is that you've endured, I'm sure it was painful, and it might always be a traumatic memory for you.

But guess what?

You got through it.

In fact, you've gotten through every single hard thing that's ever been thrown your way. Life is full of ups and downs, unexpected things, and sometimes hard seasons. But if you stay patient and get through the difficult days, eventually they come to an end. You make it to the other side feeling stronger and more knowledgeable.

Just think about all the hard things you've ever gone through. Right now, take a moment and think about it. Now, once you've done that, think about this next: *You're freaking amazing.*

Seriously, kid, you're pretty badass. I don't mind cursing here because I think it's totally appropriate. You've been through so many things and you wouldn't be able to do that if you weren't the strong, badass kid that I know you are. You, my friend, are resilient and brave and fearless and driven. You're smart and inspiring and powerful and you can do absolutely anything you set your mind to.

I know you might find this to be cheesy and think that I'm just here hyping you guys up. And yes, don't get me wrong, I *do* want to be your biggest cheerleader, but I really do mean it when I say you can do absolutely anything. I remember people always telling me that when I was younger and I thought it sounded ridiculous. The truth is, you *can* do absolutely anything. Maybe not right now at this very moment, *but you can do anything in time when you focus on personal development.* That was the piece that was missing for me.

Personal growth is one of the most amazing concepts that has undoubtedly changed my life. I'm not sure why our education system hasn't implemented personal growth into our high school years, but I believe one day it will be. Teens struggle with vast insecurities, their self-esteem, self-doubt, and poor body image. So why wouldn't we focus on developing those skills and building teens' self-image?

I think we all need to change this together. Personal development is going to make such a difference in your life that it's going to feel like it smacked you in the face. (But in a good way, of course!) I promise, it's worth it.

Everything great in life comes with practice. You don't start the beginning of your sports career as the most valuable player. You have to practice over and over again to master your skill sets. You don't begin a career in art the first time you sit down to draw a picture. It might take years and years of practice to perfect your artistic abilities. You don't just wake up one day and know how to apply makeup on your face. You have to practice it over and over again until you get the hang of it.

The reality is that your confidence, your body image, and your positive mindset work the exact same way. You don't begin your teen years being the most confident person in the world. You practice over and over again until you master your skillsets.

With that said, you need to dedicate a small chunk of time every day to personal development just like you would with anything else that you want to perfect. It doesn't need to be an annoying, cheesy, time-consuming process though, so we're going to dig into the details below.

I want you teens to know just how freaking amazing you are. You're special and kind. You're important and valuable. You're complex and unique. You guys are so dang stinkin' amazing that I'd run out of pages if I tried to list all the words I wanted to add. So, let's jump in. I'm determined to help you see what I see.

Routines Are Essential to Being Awesome

If you think back on your younger years, like preschool and kindergarten, you might think about some of the activities you guys did on a daily basis. When I think of those years, I think of arts and crafts and those not-so-comfy toddler mats that we used to nap on in daycare. But one of the biggest things I remember from that time of my life was that in preschool, we were on a pretty tight schedule. We were booked for activities the first hour, then snacks the second. We had naptime in the early afternoon, then lunch, and more activities after that. Adults work so hard to get young kids on a strict routine because that's how our bodies and minds work best. When kids know the routine, they're not worried about what's coming next because they'll already know. Their bodies adapt to the routines too, getting hungry when snack time is near and sleepy when it's time for a nap. They're comfortable throughout the day because it's a consistent schedule.

The weird thing is that the desire for a routine never changes. For some reason, as we transition from our kindergarten years and into elementary school, we start spending more time with friends, we get less sleep, and we get a bit more independent to do some of the things we want to do. And suddenly, routines don't seem nearly as important as they did a few years earlier. And then as you continue through middle school and high school, many of you stay up until midnight, eat at random times throughout the day, and the thought of a routine has basically been thrown out the window.

I honestly believe that just like Math, Science, English and Social Studies, Routines should be a class in elementary school, so our young minds are molded early. Unfortunately, that isn't the case though. So I'm going to stress the importance of it here.

We've established many times throughout this book that your teen years can feel stressful, overwhelming, and just flat out difficult. When you have a day that's disorganized and unpredictable, you're increasing your anxiety and the chances for things to get harder.

When you have a structure to your day, you're organized, you're focused, and you're comfortable because you know what events are coming up next. Routines bring on a sense of control because when you create your schedule, you own your day. You feel in control, which helps to get past the things that you can't control. Teens always tell me, "I don't have enough time to do that." And I'm here to tell you that's a bold face lie. We all have 24 hours in a day, but it's up to you what you plan to do with your time.

You have homework to do? Schedule it in. You want to get exercise tomorrow? Schedule it in. Do you want to spend time with friends? Schedule it in. You want to practice that instrument you bought last week? Schedule it in. You want to learn how to cook? Schedule it in.

I told you earlier in the chapter that in time, you can do anything you possibly want to do in your life and I really do mean that. Developing a routine that works for you is going to be the key to unlocking your full potential. You'll be well rested, more productive, and more focused throughout your day when you live on your own terms and on a schedule that you love.

Gratitude Is an Everyday Thing

Now that you're creating an amazing routine for yourself, one of the things you're going to need to pencil in everyday is time for gratitude. And don't roll your eyes or shut the book or give up on me now. We're almost done here and I promise this isn't going to be some stupid thing about flowers and daisies and the sun shining bright and oh, happy day!

No, it's not. Our days can be long and hard sometimes. But having a moment of intentional thought every single day can help bring you back to a sense of bliss and happiness.

I recently listened to a podcast with John Maxwell and he mentioned that every time he goes on vacation with his grandchildren, he asks them at the end of the trip these same two questions: What did you love and what did you learn?

When I first heard that, I thought, *Wow, what simple questions and yet, they're so powerful to reflect on your trip.* But then, my brain kept going and I thought, *If only teens asked themselves this every day.*

You shouldn't just think about what you loved and learned at the end of a vacation because many of us don't have the opportunity to go on vacation. And even if you do, vacation is often a time for fun things and happy moments so it's easy to find parts of the trip that you loved. I think the moments where you really learn something are in the hard times of your ordinary days. Those are the teaching moments and the things we need to focus on.

Our world continues to get crazier and busier, and obstacles pop up and distract us every single day. By asking yourself these questions on a daily basis allows you to be more present, live in the moment, and be grateful for your experiences. "What did I love today and what did I learn today?" You can even shorten it and say, "What did I love? What did I learn?"

After this chapter, I want you to incorporate gratitude questions into your daily routine. You don't have to write them down and get a gratitude journal if you don't want to. (Although, for my writer friends, you might love it!) Instead, at the end of each night, when you crawl into bed, put your phone down and ask yourself those questions: What did I love? What did I learn?

Have a brief conversation with yourself. It can be short or long, it doesn't really matter because you're the only one who's going to hear it. But it's so important to reflect on each day and acknowledge the things that went well and the things that maybe didn't go so well that you could learn from. There's no right or wrong. There's no shame or guilt. You're just processing, reflecting, and expressing gratitude for the things you loved and learned.

I'm not going to beat around the bush for this one, I'm going to give it to you straight.

Your self-talk really needs to change. Seriously, it needs to be upgraded asap.

I hear so many teens on a daily basis say things like "I can't because I'm not one of those kids" or "I'm just not pretty enough" or "I'm not good at exercise" or "I can't because of my diagnosis" and a million other things that my ears don't like to hear.

I don't know who told you that you're not pretty enough or fit enough or strong enough or smart enough or good enough, but that person was wrong. And you need to stop telling yourself these horrible lies. You're worth more than gold, kid, but you need to see that for yourself. No one else can make you see that. Your value comes from within you.

External appearances will change over the course of your life. You might get taller or stronger, maybe bigger, or thinner. You might dye your hair or cut your hair off. You might change your clothes or paint your nails. You might wear glasses or get a nose ring. You might get some tattoos or wear some fancy jewelry. Your external appearances are not permanent. I promise you they will change.

Who you are on the inside is lifelong. That person is your best friend and should be your biggest cheerleader (Maybe even bigger than me or your parents!) I'm sure you wouldn't talk down to your friends or your siblings, so why would you talk down to yourself?

You need to start talking yourself up. When you speak to yourself, speak kindly with positive thoughts. If negative thoughts pop up, change them immediately. Don't even bother to say them out loud. If you need to, think of me in your head shouting about how beautiful your soul is. And I'm serious, I'm probably screaming because my volume is always turned up. I'm a pretty loud person if you want to know the truth. And I love that about myself because it's who I am.

If you want to accomplish something, stop saying, "I can't do that." Change your verbiage and rephrase the sentence to "I haven't learned that yet."

YET is a powerful word, my friend, because it tricks your brain into believing that you're going to learn it. You just haven't yet, but you will. And once you believe that truth, it's likely you're going to learn how to do it.

Imagine a toddler who's just learning how to walk. If they gave up after their first try and thought, *Well, I'll never be able to do that,* then none of us would know how to walk around on two legs. We'd all be crawling around like a bunch of weirdos.

When we're toddlers, we feel invincible and determined to learn everything. Unfortunately, something changes between our toddler years and teen years. Many of us take on fixed mindsets and adapt negative self-images.

I want you to go back to your toddler years when you were unbelievably curious about the world. Go back to the time when you wanted to learn how to do something and you dove in without any fears. Talk yourself up and believe that you can do anything because the truth is, you can.

According to Mel Robbins, the odds of you being born were 1 in 400 trillion. Do you realize how insane that number is? There was a 1 in 400 trillionth of a chance that you would even be born! How could you ever doubt yourself? You've done the most amazing thing that you

Epilogue

Well, that was exciting.

You finally got through it, kid. It wasn't too bad, was it?

Those are the tips and tricks that I hope you will utilize during your teen years. As I mentioned earlier, I desperately wish I had a mentor who shared some of this information with me earlier in life. It definitely would have saved me from some embarrassing moments and helped guide me through some difficult seasons.

What makes me so excited about this book too is that most of this information is not based on my opinions. These strategies have been proven time and time again through trial and error. These tools have helped teens in the past and I'm confident they will continue to help millions of teens in the future.

They've helped me, Nicole, the author of this book, even after my teen years and into adulthood. This is the foundation of personal growth. It's the process of realizing that you are in control of your entire life, your future, and everything in between. You have more potential than you'll ever know and you have the power to reach it by continuously enhancing your quality of life.

It all starts with you, kid.

But the entire purpose of this book was to help you kickstart your personal development journey. I wanted to put all the strategies in one easy place as a guide for your success. I truly believe if you implement these tools into your life throughout your teen years (and even long after), you will show up every day as the best possible version of you (even on days when you don't feel like you are).

Now, here's one last tip. If you're an eager beaver like me and you read through the whole book at once, that's great! But I don't want you to feel overwhelmed going back through the book trying to pick out which tools you should implement in your life first. Make it easy on yourself and go chapter by chapter. And certainly don't try to add them in simultaneously. Remember, you can do everything in the world, but you can't do it all at the same time. Don't overwhelm yourself or you'll set your path up for failure. Focus on one topic for a few weeks first and then when you feel confident enough to add another one, do it. But start with one.

Then, continue practicing these strategies throughout the rest of your teen years. I believe the future holds something truly amazing for you, my friend. I know because I've seen it. I see it all the time and I've lived through it. As a teen, it's hard to see what great things lie beyond high school and it's even harder to see what lies beyond college. But when I was a teen, I was able to see something that seemed small at the time. I saw a successful, calmer, more graceful, loving, kind, determined, helpful version of myself and I just need some guidance and a map to tell me how to get there.

So, now I'm holding my hand out to you. I'm giving you some guidance and it's your turn now.

Look into your future, right now. What does your life look like in five years from now? Are you still in school? Or are you in college maybe? Do you have the same friends? Are you working at a part-time job? Or a full-time job maybe? What does your life look like? Are you happy with that vision? Or are you unhappy? What do you want it to look like? Do you have to make a change in order to get the future that you desire? These are all the questions I want you to ask yourself as you look into your future. There might be many other questions that pop up into your head too, and that's OK. Do all the soul searching you need in order to create the amazing vision you desire. The important thing is that you recognize you're in control. You're in control of your emotions, your behaviors, your thoughts, your future. Be the captain of your ship and take control of the wheel. Steer the boat where you desire.

This is just the beginning of your story, my friend. You have a long way to go so don't stop now. Only look back to see how far you've come.

Together, we've talked about your feelings and how they're totally valid. You're allowed to feel however you want to feel and so is everyone else around you. The emotions you feel are a part of your human experience and you should embrace them while giving yourself grace at the same time.

We've also talked about being a better listener and that everyone wants to be heard. We've talked about anxiety and how you're stronger than the anxiety you feel. We've covered diagnoses and how you should never let yours limit you.

We've talked about making your health a priority. You should have a balanced nutritional diet and get the proper amount of sleep at night. Movement is medicine. You need to be physically active and get outside in the fresh air and the sunlight in order to maintain your physical health *and* your emotional health as well. This chapter is so important that maybe you should even go back and read it twice.

We've talked about daydreaming, visualization, and how the things you speak will manifest itself into existence. We've talked about balance and having fun and being a teen, but having self-discipline because moderation is key. We've talked about your identity and I know, I know, it's still a weird thing, but it's important to understand who you are and who you want to be. We've talked about your values, your self-worth, and how you should never compare yourself to anyone else.

We've talked about change, its inevitability, and how growth is pretty freaking awesome. If you can't look back on your past years and laugh at who you used to be, then, kid, you probably haven't grown enough. We've talked about setting routines, social media breaks, and giving yourself time to rest. We've talked about how sometimes, adults just don't get it. And things get hard, but challenges make you stronger and everything in life eventually passes.

I think the most important one of all though is that we've covered how freaking amazing you are. And I mean it too. You're unique and authentic and there's quite literally no one other soul in the world like you.

So I hope through our journey together that you've gained some knowledge that you can carry forth and use as tactical knowledge in the future. I hope you can take some of this wisdom and share it with your friends and help them become the best version of themselves too. I hope that you will continue learning and growing and having an open mind to experience the new world ahead of you. I hope that you take these strategies and apply them to your life because now you have a whole new perspective.

I want you to go out and do whatever it is that lights your soul on fire. And I hope that you will continue to address anything in your life that may need to be addressed. I hope you do it with patience, flexibility, and confidence. I hope that you will continue to nurture and enhance the relationships you have with your family and friends.

It takes work to see things that are not yet present. So believe in your ability to get there. Be bold. Be confident. Be humble. Be coachable. Be flexible. Be consistent. Be hungry. And for heaven's safe, be a freaking teen. It can be an amazing time if you let it. You're going to live an amazing life, kid. So be persistent. Stay focused. Set realistic goals and I promise, you will win.

Printed in the USA
CPSIA information can be obtained
at www.ICGtesting.com
LVHW080747040823
754031LV00015B/631

9 781638 297635